The Budding Legacy

A celebration of a British 'grass-roots' invention

Written and compiled by Chris Biddle

Design and Artwork: Martin Hebditch

Published by:
Chris Biddle Media

The Budding Legacy

First published in 2015 by:
Chris Biddle Media
12 Kingfisher Close
SALISBURY, Wiltshire SP2 8JE

www.chrisbiddlemedia.co.uk

© Chris Biddle 2015

All rights reserved. No part of this publication may be reproduced or transmitted in any form or by any means, electronic, mechanical, including photocopy, recording or any information storage and retrieval system, without written permission from the publishers.

A catalogue record of this book is available from the British Library

ISBN 978-0-9932553-0-4

Disclaimer
The author and publisher do not accept any responsibility in any manner whatsoever for any error or omission, or any loss, damage, injury, adverse outcome, or liability of any kind incurred as a result of the use of any of the information contained in this book.

Acknowledgments
The author gratefully acknowledges the help of the many contributors and sources used throughout the book who are listed in more detail on page 114. In particular thanks are due to the following companies who have supported the publication of The Budding Legacy:

Allett Mowers (division of Turfmech Ltd)
Briggs and Stratton Corporation
Countax Ltd
Ransomes Jacobsen Ltd

Printed by The Manson Group, St Albans AL3 6PX

Gleneagles, venue for 2014 Ryder Cup

CONTENTS

FOREWORD: David Withers	8 – 9
INTRODUCTION	10-11
IN PRAISE OF LAWNS	12-13
STROUD: Birthplace of the lawnmower	14-17
EDWIN BUDDING: A complex genius	18-21
TIMELINE: Evolution of the lawnmower	22-25
THE WAY WE MOW: Our character revealed	26-27
A CUT ABOVE: Hours of perfection mowing	28-31
LEGACY SERIES No 1: Shay Rotoscythe	33
CUT GRASS Our favourite smell	34-37
PICTURE GALLERY	38
LEGACY SERIES No 2: Allen Scythe	39
MOWERS FOR ALL A bewildering choice	40-43
LEGACY SERIES No 3: Flymo	45
BRITISH LAWNMOWER MUSEUM	46-53
THE COLLECTORS: Restoring history	54
LEGACY SERIES No 4: JP Mowers	55
READY, STEADY, MOW: Top athletes compete	56
LEGACY SERIES No 5: Atco mowers	57
WIMBLEDON: Turf perfection	58-61
WHERE THE ACTION IS: The role of groundsmen	62-68
LEGACY SERIES No 6: Hayterette	69
LIONS AND THE LAWNS: Greening of Trafalgar Square	70-71
PROFILE: Briggs & Stratton	72-73
LEGACY SERIES No 7: Suffolk mowers	75
LEGACY SERIES No 8: British Anzani	76
BUDDING AND RANSOMES: 150 years connected	77-81
FAST MOWERS: Man and machines	82-87
LEGACY SERIES No 9: Dennis Mowers	88
QUOTES: Lawns, mowing and the meaning of life	89-92
LEGACY SERIES No10: Lloyds mowers	93
PROFILE: Allett Mowers	94-95
LAWNMOWERS AND ADVERTISING: Through the ages	96-101
PROFILE: Countax	102-103
EARN YOUR STRIPES: Mowing as an art form	104-105
BUDDING AND BEER: A name immortalised	106-107
LOOK NO HANDS: The march of the robots	108-112
PERENNIAL: The horticultural charity	113
ACKNOWLEDGEMENTS	114

The Budding Legacy

FOREWORD

Ransomes machines prepare world famous golf courses such as Pebble Beach, California.

Our heritage

August 31st in the year 1830 was a momentous day for Edwin Beard Budding when he lodged the patent for 'a new combination and application of machinery for the purpose of cropping or shearing the vegetable surface of lawns, grass-plats and pleasure grounds'.

Thus, the world's first lawnmower was born and little did he know how his invention would impact the world. Two years later Ransomes of Ipswich in Suffolk were one of first companies to manufacture the Budding patent under licence.

What I find quite amazing is that over 180 years later we are still cutting grass in exactly the same way, using a rotating cylinder and a fixed bottom blade to shear the grass plant. Budding was so far ahead of his time, that we have not found a better way of maintaining fine turf.

What is equally amazing is that Ransomes mowers are still being manufactured in Ipswich to this day and that is a fact that makes me extremely proud.

From great sporting arenas, parks, formal gardens, open spaces to our own lawns at home, we are a nation infatuated with the appearance of our grassed areas. And how we love our stripes!

This book by Chris Biddle is more than just a celebration of Budding's original achievement, it looks at how the mower has progressed across the centuries and celebrates the fact that the UK is still a manufacturing centre of excellence.

It is a fitting tribute to our industry and, what's more, it's a very good read.

David Withers
President, Jacobsen

David Withers is President of Jacobsen, the turf division of US industrial group Textron Inc. Textron, who include Cessna Aircraft, Bell Helicopters and E-Z-GO off-road vehicles in the Group, bought Ransomes in 1998 to add to its Jacobsen turf machinery business, and is based in Charlotte, North Carolina with manufacturing facilities in the US and Ipswich in the UK.

INTRODUCTION

Mottisfont Abbey is a historical priory and country estate in England. Sheltered in the valley of the River Test, the property is now operated by the National Trust.

THERE has never been any doubt that the British love their lawns. They admire the precise preparation of the Wimbledon Courts, the outfield at Lords', the swathes of fairways and finely cut greens at St Andrews, the luscious turf at Ascot and the immaculate 'grass stage' at Twickenham or Wembley.

Or they simply enjoy the outdoor pleasure provided by the parks and open spaces in our towns and cities, Grass is the great escape. It provides a living and tactile surface on which to rest and play.

Freshly mown grass, particularly after summer rain, is one of the most evocative smells on the planet. Researchers have discovered that a chemical released by a mown lawn makes people feel happy and relaxed, and could prevent mental decline in old age - and a neatly cut lawn can add immense value to a house sale.

Around the world, British lawn mowing equipment is in high demand, as are the skills of talented British greenkeepers and groundsmen who are now employed by many of the world's leading golf courses and sports stadiums.

Nothing illustrates our love of grass than when the hard-standing of Trafalgar Square was covered with specially grown turf for two days. It changed the complexity, the tone and the ambience of one of the world's most recognised venues at a stroke. Londoners flocked to sit, exercise, picnic, play and gaze at a total transformation. Yet there was nothing new, no magic ingredient – just one of our most common and durable plants providing visual and tactile pleasure.

In short, we 'do' grass better than anyone else in the world. Our expertise, knowledge and equipment is recognised worldwide.

GRASS-ROOTS

And it all started in the Gloucestershire town of Stroud in the 1830's, when a young, ambitious and innovative textile engineer called Edwin Budding had his 'eureka' moment whilst setting up a machine to finely trim the 'knap' off the rough cloth on a batch of guardsmen's uniforms to ensure a fine and smooth finish.

Quite why, and how he came to connect the cylindrical reel used in the process with cutting grass, which had hitherto only been kept in check with hand-scythes, is something of a mystery. However his timing was spot-on. It was a time of increasing prosperity. The gentry were building large houses with large grass surrounds. Sport was becoming more popular, particularly tennis, cricket and golf which required well-tended playing areas.

In retrospect, Edwin Budding should justifiably be ranked alongside the other famous inventors of his age

His invention of the first lawnmower, his drive and ambition to push forward the development and testing of prototypes before building the first commercial machines barely a year later that went into straight into work was nothing short of inspirational.

Remarkably, the design of Budding's original hand push mower is still highly recognisable today. Yet what would he would think of today's development of robotic mowers, hover mowers, radio-controlled mowers or electric mowers?

He would have been just as excited now, as then. As a visionary, he would have anticipated change. He would have welcomed lateral thinking, and have embraced evolution.

This book sets out to not only recognise the often overlooked contribution of Edwin Budding in today's society, but celebrates the role that he and his successors have played to our social, sporting and cultural life. Not only in the UK but around the world.

Chris Biddle

Chris Biddle is the founder and editor of **Service Dealer**, *the UK's leading magazine for grass and farm machinery dealers now in its 27th year, and of* **Turf Pro**, *the online news and information resource for greenkeepers and groundsmen. He lives in Salisbury with wife Trish, loves cricket and has been a proud member of the MCC for over 50 years.*
www.servicedealer.co.uk
www.turfpro.co.uk

In Praise of

Lawns have been variously described as a place of sanctity, a living urban lung, an exercise space, playground, environmental relief to brick and concrete, an outdoor 'room' and somewhere to connect with nature. In truth, they are all of these. . .and more.

The British interest in lawns stretches back more than 800 years when the gardens of Henry 11 at Clarendon, Wiltshire were said to 'boast a wealth of lawns' and during the reign of Henry III in 1259 the gardens of the Palace of Westminster were recorded as being levelled with a roller and turf laid and later 'mown (with a scythe).

Grass is one of the most resilient of all plants. During the winter, the lawn can be covered in snow and frost. At any time of the year it can become flooded. It can suffer damaging assaults on its surface, become disfigured, bruised and battered. In summer, lawns can turn brown in hot August sun, and yet a day or two of rain and the verdant green returns, as if by magic.

A lawn is the seasonal indicator. The sound of mowers on the first warm afternoon in Spring signifying the end to human winter hibernation. A portent of garden chairs being unfolded, the barbecue cleaned, edges clipped and the space readied for the time when we can relax, stretch out and smell nature.

Lawns are pliable. They respond to feet and touch in a way that no artificial surface ever can. In his book, The Forgiveness of Nature, Graham Harvey says *"To step onto turf is to step out of the everyday. Grass represents liberty.*

A day or two of rain and the verdant green returns, as if by magic.

In Praise of Lawns

Lawns

By stepping onto grass, we temporarily reject the ordered world of human affairs and take a brief walk along the edge of the infinite".

Lawns are therapeutic. The Gospel According to Zen *"Sitting quietly, doing nothing, Spring comes, and the grass grows by itself"* Grass is the great escape, whether on the lawn, in the park, on the golf course or cricket ground

But lawns do not just happen. As millions of readers of the books produced by best selling author Dr David Hessayon know only too well, good lawns demand attention They must be watered, scarified, de-thatched and fed In short, they need 'TLC', whilst at the same time they provide the opportunity for exercise and outdoor activity. Mowing the lawn can be beneficial for mind and body. It can be contemplative, relaxing and yet a challenge.

> *Grass represents liberty. By stepping onto grass, we temporarily reject the ordered world of human affairs.*
> *Graham Harvey*

The English are universally acknowledged to be the lawn creators, coming up with most of the sports or games based on grass, as well as inventing the original grass-cutting machines. The British lawn is a unique, complex and yet modest creation – and remains as much a symbol of our country as fish and chips, the Union Jack and the Houses of Parliament.

In Praise of Lawns

Stroud:
Birthplace of the lawnmower

Stroud viewed from Rodborough Common

The town of Stroud is the capital of the south western Cotswolds and located at the divergence of the five Golden Valleys, named after the monetary wealth created in the processing of wool from a plentiful supply of water power.

In the Middle Ages the Cotswolds were well known throughout Europe as the source of some of the best wool. The area was ideal for sheep, so the Abbeys and monasteries raised huge flocks of the 'Cotswold Lions', large native sheep with golden long fleeces. Local merchants became rich and spent a great deal of money on the wool churches as well as building fine houses.

At that time, the wool trade accounted for 50% of England's economy.

The area around Stroud had several natural aids to its success in the cloth industry. Its proximity to the sheep raised on the Wolds, the fast flowing rivers and streams that could power mills capable of processing raw wool and finishing the cloth, and the district's geology, which provided an abundant supply of Fuller's Earth.

Fuller's Earth greatly facilitated the stripping of natural oils from the wool, making the cloth easier to dye. The consistent dye quality and fineness of Stroud's cloths gained the area international fame.

During the heyday of the wool trade the River Frome powered 150 mills, turning Stroud into a major centre for the production of cloth.

Stroud's cloth industry was at its peak between 1790 and 1830 and the industrial wealth and the technological innovation and investment in quality architecture that accompanied it – brought the booming area greater status and respect. In particular Stroudwater scarlet, a lovely rich dye, became famous throughout Europe for military uniforms.

With the town becoming an important industrial and trading location during the nineteenth century, it badly needed transport links, relying as it did on a canal network in the form of the Stroudwater Navigation and the Thames and Severn Canal both of which survived until the early 20th century.

In 1845 the Great Western Railway line running to Cheltenham arrived in Stroud from Swindon. For the first time, Stroud had a reliable and fast link to the capital. The new railway had an immediate effect on Stroud's previous transport communications. The stagecoach ceased to run soon after the opening and the Thames and Severn Canal's receipts dropped by a third in 4 years. But, because the railway ran too high above the valley floor to be of use to the mills, which still used canal wharves for the delivery of their coal, local trade on the Thames and Severn continued.

Many of the old mills have fallen into disrepair

But long distance trade was harder hit. The Midland Railway Company arrived in the Stroud district with the opening in 1867 of a line between Stonehouse and Nailsworth and immediately the new railway line had great consequences for the mills to the south and west of Stroud.

Sidings from the main line led directly to the mills, allowing a far cheaper and easier method of transporting goods and coal.

Bucking the downward turn in the cloth industry, the Midland railway brought prosperity to the mills along its length. Another wave of rebuilding and expansion ensued, but unfortunately did not last.

By the end of the 19th century the Stroud valleys' cloth trade started to decline, having finally been beaten by competition from Yorkshire.

Many of the mills closed or were adapted to other industries. The manufacture of needles, pins, machine parts, bobbins, reels, umbrella handles and walking sticks came to the area – as did the manufacturing of farm machinery and equipment.

> *The wool trade accounted for 50% of England's economy*

AN ENGINEERING HUB

Despite the downturn in the cloth trade, a number of engineering enterprises had sprung up in and around Stroud during the 19th century. Thrupp Mill and was a cloth mill until 1828 when John Ferrabee, an iron founder, made extensive alterations and it became the Phoenix Ironworks.

One of the early Stroud built Danarm chainsaws in the Museum

The Ferrabees were noted for their production of cloth making machines, water wheels, agricultural machinery and steam engines – and it was here that Edwin Budding came up with his idea for a lawnmower in 1830 and for several years became a manufacturing centre for Budding's new machine.

In later years, Phoenix Iron Works was also to be the home to a development centre for Lister Petter engines. RA Lister & Company had been founded in nearby Dursley by Sir Robert Ashton in 1867.

Initially the company produced agricultural machinery but after the invention of the internal combustion engine, it became an important producer of petrol engines for sheep shearing equipment and other farm equipment.

In the 1920s and 30s, Listers employed over 2000 people, and with diesel engines now introduced to the range, was producing over 600 engines a week.

Post war, and as competition and labour costs increased, Lister found it impossible to return to the heydays of the 1930s, and in 1965 was acquired by Hawker Siddeley, who had previously bought its main rival Petter, the Yeovil based engine maker who had founded the Westland Aircraft Factory in 1915.

In April 2014, Lister Petter went into administration, but was bought by Birmingham based EGL Group which operates the company from a headquarters in Dubai. However, it meant the end of over 150 years of manufacturing tradition in Dursley and the surrounding area.

Another company with a long engineering tradition in Stroud, T H & J Daniels was founded by Thomas Daniels in 1840 and became a significant engineering and foundry business in the area. In 1916, Daniels bought the Trusty Engine business, and in 1941 combined with a designer J Clubley-Armstrong to make a chainsaw, which it branded Danarm.

The first saws were powered by Villiers 2-stroke engines, from 80cc up to 350cc. The larger models were capable of taking cutter bars up to 7ft in length! Many of the early saws were supplied to War Office specification for use in jungle battle areas.

In 1954 the best selling DANARM DD8F Saw was

The restored Ebley Mill is home to Stroud District Council

introduced, incorporating the Villiers 98cc '8F' 2-stroke engine. The saw weighed about 28lb and was fitted with a diaphragm carburettor which enabled the saw to be used easily by one man at any angle. In the 1960's and 1970's DANARM developed their own 125cc, 110cc, 71cc and 55cc engines. Danarm saws became much lighter in weight as magnesium castings were used extensively for the larger components.

Manufacturing ceased in 1984, and the company started importing and distributing other garden machinery products, including cultivators, brushcutters, hedgetrimmers and lawnmowers, mainly sourced from the Far East.

The Danarm name remains today through its importing and distribution base at Nailsworth near Stroud.

STROUD TODAY

Even today, Stroud is very much a working town, and one which doesn't need its heritage in order to survive. Whilst some of the old mills have been converted into flats, offices, and commercial concerns, just two continue to make cloth. No longer the so-called Stroudwater Scarlet used for military uniforms, but high-quality felt for snooker tables – and for tennis balls, which neatly links Budding's invention of the lawnmower to the world famous All England Lawn Tennis Club at Wimbledon.

At the charming, Museum in the Park in the heart of Stroud, the connection is well-made, with a sign that proudly proclaims WITHOUT STROUD, NO WIMBLEDON.

The Museum is set in the beautiful grounds of Stratford Park in a Grade II listed 17th Century wool merchant's mansion house. With over 4,000 objects on display, including dinosaur bones, historical paintings and many artifacts, the collection tells the fascinating story of the Stroud District's rich and diverse history.

For good reason, Stroud is often refered to as the 'Covent Garden of the Cotswolds'. There is much to engage and interest a visitor to Stroud. Not simply its industrial heritage but through strong arts and literary connections with the likes of Laurie Lee (Cider with Rosie), best selling author Jilly Cooper and a host of artists and sculptors such as Lynn Chadwick and Damien Hirst who have made the town their home and workplace.

Stroud's Museum in the Park

Edwin Budding:
A complex genius

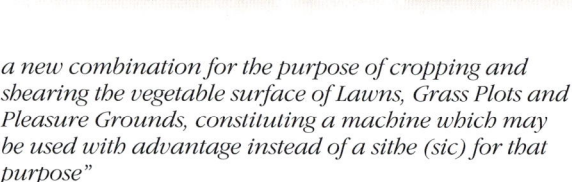

There are only a few facts about the life of Edwin Beard Budding of which we can be absolutely certain. First that he was born 25 August 1796, the illegitimate son of a farmer. In the 1820s he worked as an engineer and machinist at the Phoenix Iron Works at Thrupp near Stroud. This was a former mill that local businessman John Ferrabee had leased and subsequently gained permission to convert to an engineering works. Here Ferrabee manufactured machines for the cloth trade, water wheels, steam engines and farm machinery.

In 1830, Budding stumbled across a method of cutting grass mechanically, a task that was hitherto undertaken by scythe. On 18th May of the same year, he signed a formal Agreement with Ferrabee acknowledging that he, Edwin Beard Budding *"had invented and applied a new combination for the purpose of cropping and shearing the vegetable surface of Lawns, Grass Plots and Pleasure Grounds, constituting a machine which may be used with advantage instead of a sithe (sic) for that purpose"*

The essence of the Agreement was that Ferrabee would be the 'money-man' and supply the cash needed to make the machine a marketable reality. All the initial profits would go to Ferrabee until his original outlay was covered. Thereafter, the pair would split the profits equally.

A few months later, in October 1830, Budding and Ferrabee applied for, and were granted, a patent which described the invention in minute detail including specifications of the drive wheels, pinions, gears, cogs, cutting cylinder and so on.

From there, the story embarks on a growing commercial future for Budding's invention through a process of manufacturing licences to others.

At some unspecified time, Budding's relationship with Ferrabee appears to have cooled a little and he moved the short distance to Dursley where was to work with George Lister, the second son of the founder of the celebrated agricultural engineers, R A Lister of Dursley. Together the

Edwin Budding: A complex genius

pair worked on developing new carding machines for the textile industry, machines which would separate fibres before the spinning process.

Thereafter, Budding lived a quiet life in a modest cottage until his death on 25 September 1846. He was survived by his widow, Elizabeth, who died in 1874.

SPANNERS, GUNS – AND MOWERS

But who was the real Edwin Budding? What motivated him to create of a piece of machinery that would having a lasting impact on our society across the ages? Why grass cutting?

It is clear that Budding was no ordinary engineer. He had an enquiring and open mind towards engineering-based inventions. Sometime in the late 1820s, he came up with the idea of the adjustable spanner as a result having to make frequent adjustments to the forged bolt heads on cloth making machinery. Whereas several designs were forthcoming at that time in the United States for the adjustable wrench, the term English Key was used to describe the type of tool that Budding and another British inventor Richard Clyburn had designed as a universal size spanner. Once again, Budding was the ideas man, Ferrabee the producer. Early advertising described the tool as Ferrabee's Budding Spanner.

There was Budding's gun – a pepper box revolver. It seems that Budding had thoughts on how he could improve on Samuel Colt's pistol. In all he made three models, all with five chambers, beautifully engineered with brass barrels. He manufactured only a small quantity, possibly less than 50 in all, but those remaining have a considerable rarity value. A Budding gun sold at a London auction house a few years ago for £6600.

But as it turned out, adjustable spanners and exclusive revolvers were to become a side-show to Budding's real claim to fame.

It is an accepted notion that Buddings 'eureka' moment for a machine to mechanically shear grass came whilst he was involved in engineering a machine that would shear off the rough nap on the cloth used for guardsman's uniforms so they had a smooth finish.

However, the basis of his new application had its roots in another development that had taken place some years earlier, again at the Phoenix Iron Works.

Early textile workers had used a clumsy and heavy-to-use set of shears developed originally in Holland. The Leiden shears (called after the town once the hub of Dutch cloth making) were used to remove the rough and lumpy bits from a length of cloth. They could be brutal and dangerous.

In 1815, John Lewis, son of the owner of Brimscombe Mill which adjoined Thrupp Mill, invented a new-style napping machine which employed a horizontal blade that could be rolled across the surface of the cloth. It worked better, and more safely, than the Leiden Shears, but still had its limitations.

Lewis had asked Ferrabee to manufacturer his new napping machine, but was still not happy that the design was right. He subsequently came up with a better solution that would involve twisting the horizontal blade into a spiral which moved against a secondary fixed blade to achieve a continuous cutting action. That was the 'trigger' for Budding's realisation

Edwin Budding: A complex genius

of a new use for the machine. It is probable that he had worked on Lewis's prototypes and on the alternative spiralled reel in place of the original horizontal blade.

Quite how he made the connection, or indeed whether it was a solution to an opportunity that had been nagging away at him for some while, we'll never know.

However, these were changing times. In the countryside, there was massive unrest amongst farm workers as mechanisation started to take hold. Newly developed threshing machines were targeted and destroyed by rural gangs in what were termed the Swing Riots.

Across the country, manual tasks were being replaced by machines. And that was as true in the textile and cloth trade as it was in farming.

But it was also a time of growing prosperity – and yes, more leisure time as a result of greater mechanisation. The local gentry, including mill owners built large houses surrounded by an expanse of lawn. Sports and pastimes like cricket, golf and tennis were becoming more popular. The Royal Aberdeen Golf Course was built in 1780, whilst Thomas Lord had founded his famous cricket ground in London in 1814, some 15 years earlier.

The word 'lawn' was not new. William Shakespeare set a scene in *As You like It* on a 'Lawn before the Dukes palace'. Nor was the word 'mowing'. Except that prior to Budding's invention, 'mowing' refered to keeping the grass in check with a hand-scythe.

Adjoining the Phoenix Iron Works were a number of meadows, laying between the factory and the river. It is entirely possible that these were tended by a scythe, and that Budding had noted that the grass was only being cut during wet weather or at a dewy dawn.

His machine was different. It could be used when the grass was dry and the sun was at its highest, in sociable hours and by anybody in the family, rather than hire an unskilled labourer.

In other words, it was to be a social change as much as a mechanical advance.

For two or three years, Budding and Ferrabee perfected their invention, often it is believed testing prototypes in the dead of night, either in case they be laughed at or possibly to stop others stealing a march on them.

The time-scale from prototype to marketable machine was extraordinarily swift. No more than two years.

Thereafter, Budding appeared to take a back-seat. His place in history assured, but with no apparent wealth or fame as his legacy. A complex character for sure. A genius? Of that there is no doubt. An engineering celebrity? Hardly. A place in history? Certainly.

In a later era, the pairing of Budding and Ferrabee might have been a Marks and Spencer, Mercedes-Benz, even a Ransomes, Sims & Jefferies. Names for ever joined in everyday language. But no, their professional union was relatively short.

It was to be a social change as much as a mechanical advance

As a parting shot though, much is made of the engineering acumen of Edwin Budding, his technical skill and innovative mind. What is often overlooked is the design itself, the aesthetic look that has lasted a lifetime.

Search in garden sheds up and down the land, and you will find thousands of mowers made in more recent times that eerily resemble Budding's original machine. The elegant curvature of the handles, the precision cutting cylinder, the sturdy metal rear roller and flattening wooden front rollers – all held together and operated by series of gears, cogs and chains.

There are surely few inventions over the past two centuries that have changed so much in operational advancements as the Budding Lawnmower, but which still retain their basic look and design concept.

Edwin Budding: A complex genius

TIMELINE
How the lawnmower

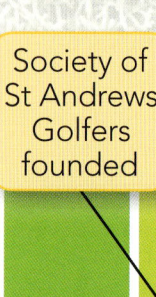

Society of St Andrews Golfers founded

Thomas Lord builds his cricket ground at present site

First manufacturing licence granted to J R and A Ransome of Ipswich

Both Thomas Green of Leeds and Alexander Shanks of Arbroath took further licences

Shanks develop mower designed to be pulled by a horse (*coining the phrase Shanks Pony*)

1766 1814 1832 1840 1854

1796 1830 1834 1846 1859

Edwin Budding born

Budding invents the lawnmower

Royal and Ancient Golf Club formed at St Andrews

Edwin Budding dies at the age of 50

Thomas Green improves Budding mower by adding a rake

ndustry has evolved

First Gentlemen's Singles lawn tennis played at Wimbledon

Celebrated cricketer W G Grace endorses Ransomes motor mower

First groundsman engaged for Lords Cricket Ground

W J Stephenson-Peach designs first petrol-driven mower

Atco Mowers and Qualcast Mowers both founded in Derby

1865   1877   1896   1906   1920

1868   1893   1902   1908   1921

All England Club formed at Wimbledon, mainly for croquet

First steam powered mower built by Leyland

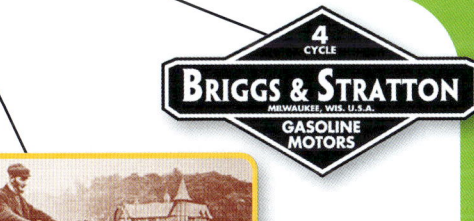
Ransomes acquire patent for petrol mower and commence production

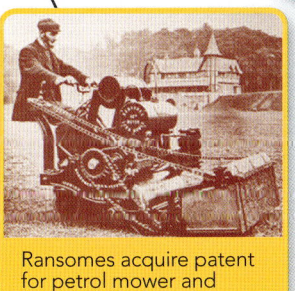

Atco Standard becomes first mass-produced petrol powered lawnmower

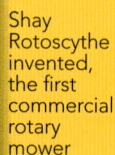

Shay Rotoscythe invented, the first commercial rotary mower

Doug Hayter makes his first mower in his shed in Hertfordshire

Mountfield Mowers founded by Gerry Cohen and Denis Selby

Karl Dahlman invents the Flymo Hover Mower

1922 1933 1946 1961 1964

Dennis Lawnmower manufactured by engineers Dennis Brothers

1926 1935 1960 1963 1965

Qualcast acquires Suffolk Lawnmowers

Allen Scythe made by Didcot company

Qualcast buys Charles H Pugh, makers of Atco mowers

World's first electric mower made by Ransomes

John Deere enters the lawnmower market

Less Bovver than a hover campaign
(Flymo v Qualcast)

First solar powered robot mower launched by Husqvarna

Allen Power Equipment closes

Bosch sell Atco tooling, drawings to Allett Mowers. Atco brand name acquired by GGP Italy Spa

Atco Qualcast acquired by Robert Bosch

Countax acquires Westwood Tractors

1985 1995 2000 2006 2011

Robotic mowers become the fastest selling sector in European market

1988 1998 2005 2010 2014

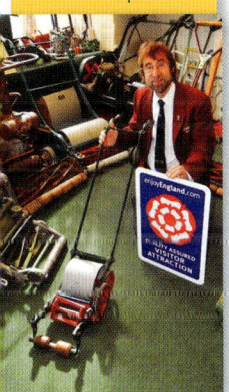
British Lawnmower Museum opens

Ransomes acquired by US group Textron Inc

Countax ride-on mower driven by Donald Campbell's grandson averaged 87.83mph over a measured mile on Pendine Sands in Wales

Toro Company buys Hayter

The Way We Mow
Stripes or a quick trim?
The way you mow can say a lot
about your character

THE way you mow your lawn may reveal secrets about your character, according to research carried out by Donna Dawson, an expert in behavioural psychology. Dawson identified four distinct personality types based solely on the ways they tackle cutting the grass.

The four groups are dubbed;

The Croquet Set: *described as obsessively neat, often workaholics.*

Nature Lovers: *Relaxed attitude about life, love and their lawns.*

The Weekenders: *Predictable lawns, predictable love lives.*

Garden Fencers: *The lawn is their social centre, they are usually romantics.*

Dawsons' research involved interviewing over 1,000 people across England. She discovered that despite growing interest in decking, gravel, water features and artificial grass, that real grass lawns were highly popular.

The largest group identified (46%) were the **Nature Lovers**. This group seldom make plans and prefer spontaneity to routine. They can be passionate lovers. Their lawns are usually in need of a good trim (presumably because they are otherwise engaged!) whilst their gardens often have weeds sprouting through.

For the **Garden Fencers** (36%), the lawn is less of a trophy and more of a venue for social interaction. They are more interested in people than plants, but they keep their lawns neat and tidy in case visitors drop by – but are not concerned by the odd weed.

The Croquet Set (12%) are identified by the precise lines on their lawns and tend to be high achievers who are only happy when their lawn is billiard table smooth with contrasting stripes – and not a weed in sight. They are likely to be workaholics who never make a move without considering the consequences, but sadly for this group, their love lives can suffer as a result of their obsessive personality.

> *Any brain-eye-hand co-ordination, like mowing the lawn, relates back to personality*

The Weekenders (6%) display an analytical approach to life problems. They count mowing the lawn amongst the week's tasks when the week's activity is over. This group tend to be predictable in other areas of their life, including romance. Their lawns are neat but lack the distinctive lines of the Croquet Set.

Commenting Donna Dawson says "Even if the way you mow your lawn is not a conscious decision, it will reveal things about you. Any brain-eye-hand co-ordination, like mowing the lawn, relates back to personality"

The survey, which was commissioned by Black & Decker, also found woman preferred a lawn with a natural appearance, whilst men tended to favour a lawn mowed expertly into stripes.

A Cut Above

How Britain's gardeners devote hours and hours to create a perfect lawn

Edwin Budding would have purred with pleasure at the dedication and commitment of Britain's gardeners to showcase his invention and produce such immaculate 'green-swards'.

For the past few years, the world's leading manufacturer of small engines for lawnmowers, Briggs & Statton, has staged a competition to find the Best Lawn in Britain. Hundreds of entries are submitted every year, and according to the judges, the standard is going up and up.

In 2012, retired doctor Chisholm Ogg was awarded the Best in Britain title for the lawn at his 19th century cottage in Long Wittenham, Oxfordshire. Dr Ogg has spent the last 14 years lovingly tending his garden for up to ten hours a day. He says "Doing the garden is my hobby and you get a nice warm feeling when you look at it. I thoroughly enjoy it"

What is surprising is that his favoured lawnmower is nearly 50 years old. Dr Ogg, a former consultant kidney specialist at Guy's Hospital, London, inherited the Hayter Ambassador mower from his mother, who bought it in the early 1960s and swears that it this trusted machine that helped see off hundreds of other entrants in the competition.

Chisholm Ogg

Meanwhile in Scotland, Andrew Moore from Kilmarnock mows his lawn every day, his efforts gaining him the Best Lawn in Scotland Award in 2013.

When Andrew and his wife Emily moved into their home 38 years ago, their five acres of land were just fields - and with four young children at the time, they initially used the land to keep ponies."As soon as the children grew out of the ponies, we knew we wanted to do more with the land. We started cutting into a bit of it to make a lawn, and then a bit more - and it just continued on"

Former insurance salesman Andrew, 76, says: "The garden is my life. There are a lot of lovely plants in it and there is something in bloom most of the year. There is a bit of everything and it is incredibly colourful. We are out here every day starting at seven in the morning until 8.30pm taking care of it. We do everything ourselves"

TV gardening personality Alan Titchmarsh says "Andrew has the best lawn you will probably ever see. He mows it every morning, and he hasn't been on holiday for 43 years! Now, I'm not saying that everyone should mow their lawns that frequently, or go that long without a holiday, but if you only cut your lawn once a fortnight, it's not going to look great"

"The more frequently you mow your lawn, the better it will look. Although Andrew mows every day, he often barely takes off anything off but dew. But the lawn is like a billiard table, and looks like it's made of velvet"

HIS AND HER LAWNS

The overall winners of Best Lawn in Britain in 2013 were in fact two lawns, both owned by Malcolm and Sandra Rogers from New Apley near Wragby in Lincolnshire.

Different in style, Malcolm's is a very formal affair with beautiful stripes and colourful borders, contrasting sharply with Sandra's wildlife meadow with walkways cut through for ease of access.

The head of the judging panel, Briggs & Stratton's Ian Small said "This is the first time we've had dual winners but Malcolm and Sandra's lawns are so innovative and demonstrate the flexibility and creativity of lawns. They are worthy winners of the competition with a combination of formality and environmental care"

Talking about his garden, Malcolm said: "It's not in my nature to neglect something, so it's been an ongoing project for about 10 years now. It's been difficult at times but I've enjoyed every second and I'm very proud of the results!" The Rogers open up their garden during the year, helping to raise money for local causes"

Each week in the growing season Malcolm and Sandra spend an estimated 10 hours each day tending their separate lawns and gardens. They have created them from natural grassland which demands them working hard throughout the year. Malcolm's three quarters of an acre lawn is the perfect place to relax after a hard day's gardening and Sandra's similarly sized meadow has flowers for almost six months of the year and is a haven of colour and wildlife

The secret of Malcolm's lawn success lies in cosseting grass to get that traditional, picture perfect striped carpet look. This unites the entire garden, setting off an array of textured blossoming trees and plants

Malcolm and Sandra Rogers

– here a fountain (a present from their son for his sixtieth birthday), there a pond; here a driftwood sculpture, there a clipped, dome-shaped shrub, and there a circle of hybrid tea roses. The odd exotic feature such as the spiky dark evergreen monkey puzzle tree contrasts his velvet smooth turf.

A pergola framing a lush green path leads to a pasture across the road, and Sandra's perhaps more contemporary 'meadow lawn'. In the Spring, it looks like normal, natural grassland, however from mid-summer it will be awash with a riot of colour, a wildlife haven of poppies, cowslips and dazzling array of wild flowers.

Lawns come in many types, shapes and sizes. Many of functional playgrounds, or simply a place to relax, but for the enthusiasts they become like a living green canvas, to be worked on, nurtured and presented as horticultural works of art.

Budding's Legacy Series

Iconic lawnmowers that have shaped the industry

NUMBER 1: Shay Rotoscythe

When it was introduced in 1933 the Shay Rotoscythe was a unique design that indicated the future of lawn mowing, becoming the first volume selling rotary mower.

The Rotoscythe was developed by Power Specialities of Maidenhead, Berkshire and was later acquired by J.E. Shay of Basingstoke, Hampshire and production of the Rotoscythe continued through the 1950s. One member of the team involved in the development of Shay mowers, Denis Selby went on to start up the successful Mountfield mower company in Maidenhead.

J. E. Shay Ltd, a large concern with major interests in materials handling, had been founded by Sir Emmanuel Kaye and John Sharp. The company owned and went on to build up the Lansing Bagnall fork lift trucks business. The inventor of the Rotoscythe was David Hamilton Cockburn, a recognised engineer who had already had patents granted to him in other engineering areas before he applied for the first "Rotoscythe" patent on 29th February 1932. That first patent was granted on 29th December 1932

Until the introduction of the Rotoscythe all successful lawn mowers had been based on the simple design of a cylinder working against a fixed knife bed to achieve the cut.

The mowers were constructed out of a non-rusting aluminium chassis, and had larger rubber tyres to help the handling – and were powered by Shay's own two-stroke engine.

BELOW LEFT: Early advertisement for the Shay Rotoscythe

BELOW RIGHT: Shay Rotoscythes were sold by dealers in good numbers. Pictured is a display at Devon dealership West Country Stanley West Ltd with Denis Selby (right) who was to later start Mountfield Mowers

What causes the freshly mown grass smell – and makes you relax?

In a recent national survey, the smell of freshly cut grass overwhelmingly came out as the Britain's favourite smell.

The whiff of newly mown grass proved vastly more popular (66%), than aftershave in second place (29%), a freshly cleaned house (20%) and baking (13%).

Researchers found that 53 per cent of people felt happy when they caught a hint of their favourite smell, while 46 per cent said it relaxed them.

SENSE OF SMELL

Smell may be a single sense but it triggers multiple sensations – memories, feelings, images, emotions. Furthermore your sense of smell is 10,000 times more sensitive than your sense of taste.

Perhaps this is why freshly brewed coffee rarely tastes as good as the initial smell, or why some cheeses taste better than they smell!

Explaining this mismatch between smell and taste, scientists claim that the act of swallowing the drink sends a burst of aroma up the back of the nose from inside the mouth, activating a "second sense of smell" in the brain that is less receptive to the flavour, causing a completely different and less satisfying sensation.

Professor Barry Smith, of the University of London, says: "We have got two senses of smell. One sense is when you inhale things from the environment into you, and the other is when the air comes out of you up the nasal passage and is breathed out through the nose."

The phenomenon is down to the fact that, although we have sensors on our tongue, eighty per cent of what we think of as taste actually reaches us through smell receptors in our nose. The receptors, which relay messages to our brain, react to odours differently depending on which direction they are moving in.

Your sense of smell is 10,000 times more sensitive than your sense of taste

"Think of a particularly smelly cheese" Professor Smith says. "It may smell like the inside of a teenager's training shoe. But once it's in your mouth, and you are experiencing the odour through the nose in the other direction, it is delicious"

"Then there is the example of when they don't match in the other direction. The smell of freshly brewed coffee is absolutely wonderful, but aren't you always just a little bit disappointed when you taste it? It can never quite give you that hit."

Nor of course, will freshly mown grass should you decide to chew on a clump to try and replicate that evocative smell.

WHAT CAUSES THE 'GRASSY' SMELL?

Grass emits volatile organic compounds normally, even without being cut. Research has shown that the amount of the compounds emitted can vary depending on light intensity and temperature. A wide range of compounds are given off, and both the intensity, and the identity of these compounds, is impacted when the plant is damaged.

The emissions increase markedly when grass is cut, and it is the production of compounds containing six carbons and oxygen that causes the fresh-cut grass smell.

So how are these compounds formed? (*Here is the scientific bit*)

When the grass is mechanically cut or damaged, by a lawnmower or otherwise, it triggers enzymes in the grass to start breaking down fats and phospholipids that are present.

This leads to the formation of linolenic and linoleic acids, which are oxidised and subsequently broken down by another enzyme. The breakdown splits the molecule into fragments which tend to contain either 12 or 6 carbon atoms. It is these fragments that lead to the 'cut grass' smell.

The key aroma compound produced by this process is

Cut Grass: Our favourite smell

(Z)-3-hexenal. The odour threshold for this compound (the amount of it that needs to be present in order for the human nose to be able to detect it) is a very low 0.25 parts per billion, which means there doesn't need to be a lot for its smell to be noticeable.

As a compound, it's quite unstable, and relatively quickly will rearrange to (E)-2-hexenal. This compound is known as leaf aldehyde, and has a higher odour threshold. Along with leaf alcohol ((Z)-3-hexen-1-ol), it is produced industrially on a large scale for use in the perfume and food technology industries.

There are a number of suggestions as to the purpose of the grass emitting these compounds when damaged. They are active against a range of bacteria, so one role they

Cut Grass: Our favourite smell

perform may be to protect the plant from bacteria and allow the cut ends to heal.

Additionally, they are also released when insects damage the plant – they may act as a 'signal' of sorts to other plants, priming them to 'switch on' defensive mechanisms, or release compounds that attract the predators of such pests.

GRASS: THE FEEL-GOOD SMELL

Researchers in Australia have discovered that a chemical released by a mown lawn makes people feel happy and relaxed, and could prevent mental decline in old age. They claim it works directly on the brain, in particular the emotional and memory parts known as the amygdala and the hippocampus.

Dr Nick Lavidis, a neuroscientist at the University of Queensland, Brisbane, came up with the idea for the perfume, named SerenaScent, after going on a forest trek in the US twenty years ago. "Three days in Yosemite National Park felt like a three-month holiday," he said. "I didn't realise at the time that it was the actual combination of feel-good chemicals released by the pine trees, the lush vegetation and the cut grass that made me feel so relaxed".

The cut grass that made me feel so relaxed

"Years later my neighbour commented on the wonderful smell of cut grass after I had mowed the lawn and it all started to click into place," he added.

Dr Lavidis said the aroma worked directly on the brain, in particular the emotional and memory parts known as the amygdala and the hippocampus. "These two areas are responsible for the flight or fight response and the endocrine system, which controls the releasing of stress hormones like corticosteroids.

"There are two types of stress. The first is when you are about to perform something or you know you are going to have to do something well. That's acute stress and can be a good form of stress.

"Bad stress is chronic stress and is associated with an increase in blood pressure, forgetfulness and a weakening of the immune system."

Students working on the Australian project found that animals exposed to the scent– which combines three chemical released when green leaves are cut – escaped damage to the hippocampus.

BRITAIN'S FAVOURITE SMELLS

1. **Cut grass**
2. **Aftershave**
3. **Freshly cleaned house**
4. **Baking**
5. **Sunday roast**
6. **Fresh flowers**
7. **Fresh linen**
8. **Hairspray**
9. **Bacon**
10. **Leather**

Source: Vileda UK

Picture Gallery Picture Gallery Picture Gallery

Drive and mow at the same time, a concept vehicle from Wolf

David Gower gets a groundsman job at his local cricket club

Manchester United get a new 'striper', head groundsman Keith Kent (centre) is now looking after the turf at Twickenham

Weatherman Ian MacCaskill on the Allen stand at Chelsea Flower Show

A fine cut at the St Andrews, the Home of Golf

Budding's Legacy Series

Iconic lawnmowers that have shaped the industry

NUMBER 2: Allen Scythe

The Allen Scythe was a throwback to Budding's era. Whereas the Budding invention was a machine to replace the scythe, Allen took the principle and applied mechanisation.

It was not really a lawn mower because its main use was to cut rough and long grass on verges and in fields, orchards and rough ground.

The most obvious difference between an Allen Scythe and a conventional mower was the way it cuts the grass. A large toothed cutting blade is slid rapidly back and forth against a similarly shaped fixed knife bed to give a scissor like action. This back and forth cutting action leads to the generic name of 'reciprocating knife' mowers.

The company who made it was formerly the Eddison and Nodding Company, which was bought by John Allen in 1897 who renamed it the Oxford Steam Plough Company, and then renamed it again to John Allen and Sons. It later became Allen Power Equipment trading from Didcot in Oxfordshire.

More than 250,000 Allen Scythes were manufactured by John Allen & Sons of Oxford between 1935 and 1973. With the slogan Wherever a Man Can Walk, an Allen Can Cut.

And although the Allen Scythe was best known as a grass cutter, it was sold not only as a tool for cutting grass but also as a central power unit that could be used with a range of attachments for a variety of other tasks around the garden, smallholding or farm.

At one time, 27 different implements and 13 optional extras were available for use with the Allen Scythe. Implements included a sawbench, horticultural plough, generator, hay sweep, rotary broom, carrier, centrifugal pump, sheep shears, gang mower and a compressor.

Allen Scythes were notoriously clumsy and cumbersome to drive. The engine runs and the clutch is engaged by releasing a lever on the handle, which often caused the mower to shoot forward, often faster than expected.

Although production ceased in 1973, Allen Scythes are popular with collectors of lawn mowers and are also still widely used by professional gardeners and private individuals who value the ability to cut long and rough grass easily.

Allen Power Equipment ceased trading in 2006.

> Wherever a Man Can Walk, an Allen Can Cut

Typical garden machinery dealer showroom

Mowers for All

Today the choice is bewildering, go to those with the 'mow-how'

Where do you go to buy a mower? There's a host of places to choose from, either big DIY stores, the internet, catalogue – or you could seek out and visit your local specialist garden machinery dealer for the best of all worlds. He'll not only show you machines of all shapes and sizes and prices – but he'll be able to help you choose a machine that is just right for you, your lawn – and your pocket.

Just as lawns and gardens come in different shapes and sizes, so their use can vary. Do you need a hard-wearing lawn for the children play or kick about or a more formal relaxing lawn? Somewhere to entertain friends, a lawn that encourages wildlife, a pasture, paddock or grass that just needs to be kept under control? Large area, small and compact, slopes or banks?

A cylinder mower for stripes, or a versatile rotary (which can still give you stripes)? Petrol engine for flexibility, electric or cordless for convenience? How long do you want

Cylinder mower with cassette system

to spend cutting the grass? Do you want it done and dusted as fast as possible, or is mowing the lawn a welcome spot of exercise and quiet contemplation?

Questions, questions, but whatever your requirement you can be sure that there is a lawnmower that is just right for you.

CYLINDER MOWERS

These were the original design by Edwin Budding, and as the name suggests, cut the grass with a cutting cylinder which operates rather like a pair of scissors. These machines are for the lawns that need to look good, because not only do they cut grass finely, but because of the roller front and back, give you that lovely striped effect that can really set off a lawn.

Most cylinder mowers come with a five or six blade cylinder, but for finer cutting such a bowling green or tennis court, then machines with 10 blades on the cylinder are usually used.

Size of cut can vary between 12" and 24" (and upwards), the wider sizes can come with a trailed seat making it into a ride-on cylinder mower. For those wanting a no-nonsense machine with the added benefit of useful exercise, there are plenty of push mowers on the market which are normally 12" or 14" cutting width.

For there, you have a choice of a petrol engine for go anywhere mowing, or electric motor which of course has to be plugged into a convenient power socket.

Over the years, the cylinder mower has increasing become a versatile tool with the availability of plug-in cassettes that will not only mow, but scarify and rake your lawn.

ROTARY MOWERS

Instead of a cylinder, rotary mowers have a single cutting blade mounted under the engine or electric motor. They are ideal where you need a good finish, but not quite the precise finish that you would get with a cylinder mower.

Rotary mowers

Rotary mowers again come with a choice of petrol engine, electric engine or a battery which usually needs to be recharged after every mowing session.

RIDE-ON MOWERS

For that ultimate mowing experience if the size of lawn permits, then there are a wide range of lawn and garden tractors on the market to suit every requirement. Some do not collect the grass, but as you go up the price scale then the sophistication increases with large capacity grass boxes which can generally be emptied without leaving the seat.

ROBOTIC MOWERS

Mowers which mow on their own without an operator are beginning to gain popularity, but are still fairly

They are available usually with four wheels which can easily be adjusted up and down depending on the height of the grass to be cut, or the length of the grass required. Hover mowers introduced into the UK by Flymo in the 1960s, also use a rotary blade, but like the hovercraft principle on which they were based, float on a cushion of air. They are extremely manoeuvrable and are particularly ideal for banks and slopes.

However, over the years many manufacturers have recognised the people in Britain love the stripes in their lawn, but want the flexibility of a rotary mower. So they have fitted a rear roller instead of the rear two wheels to provide a rolling, and thus striped effect.

Garden tractors

expensive. They operate with a rotary cutting blade, and the lawn needs to be set up to install control wires around the perimeter to stop the machine straying into flower beds or a pond!

The machines return to a docking station to recharge, but other than that are left to cut in fairly random patterns on a continual mowing cycle.

So there you have it, only a brief snapshot on how lawnmowers have developed in style and type since Edwin Budding's early machine. Today the watchword is convenience, ease of use, excellent finish and making a task that some regard as a chore, more pleasurable and even enjoyable.

WHAT SIZE MOWER?

Compare your lawn to the size of a tennis court which is 78ft (L) x 36ft (W) (24m x 11m) approx.

Half a tennis court: choose a 12" to 16" mower (30cm – 40cm)

Tennis court: 17" to 21" (42cm – 52cm)

Twice size of a tennis court: 21" to 26" (53cm – 65cm)

TWO LEADING UK GARDEN TRACTOR BRANDS

BUILT IN BRITAIN

DESIGNED FOR BRITISH LAWNS

Countax Ltd,
Countax House, Haseley Trading Estate,
Great Haseley, Oxon OX44 7PF
Telephone: 0800 597 7777

www.countax.co.uk

Budding's Legacy Series

Iconic lawnmowers that have shaped the industry

NUMBER 3: Flymo

The Flymo mower was developed in 1964 by Karl Dahlman, a Swedish inventor who took inspiration from the hovercraft that had been invented in the 1950s. It was a deceptively simple concept. The Flymo was a rotary mower with a blade that had been modified to create a downward stream of air as it turned. This lifted the mower off the grass so that it floated (like a hovercraft) across the lawn. And made it very easy to push around the lawn.

Whilst the basic idea is very simple, the Flymo is still an extremely clever piece of engineering. The blade has to turn fast enough to generate the air stream that lifts the mower off the lawn, but not too far or the blades will be too high above the grass and will not cut.

The first Flymo produced in 1965 was powered by a small petrol engine but in 1969 the company introduced its first electric model. The early Flymo electric mower, in blue and white livery, with its 15 inch cutting width was an instant success. It was inexpensive, easy to use and produced an adequate result for most casual gardeners. It was especially popular for use on small lawns because it did a quick job and required much less maintenance than conventional mowers. Its shape and lightweight design also meant that it could be hung flat against the wall thereby taking up much less room than most other types of mower.

For many, Flymo mowers changed the way they mowed the lawn. Because it floated across the lawn on a cushion of air, gardeners soon began to mow by pushing and pulling the mower back and forth in a sweeping motion.

The original Flymo could not pick up the clippings which were simply left on the lawn to decompose. Later, Flymo perfected a mechanism for collecting the clippings and many today's modern machines have these as standard.

The company became part of the Electrolux Group in 1969 and was later incorporated into the Group's Husqvana division.

Whilst Flymo has been a phenomenal success in the UK, the concept has never taken off in overseas markets to any great extent.

British Lawnmower Museum

More than 180 years of engineering excellence on show at the world's only mower museum

Southport on the north-west coast has much to commend it. Billed as England's Classic Resort, the famous Victorian seaside town boasts a fine pier, fashionable Lord Street, one of the country's largest flower shows, an Open Championship venue at Royal Birkdale – and a museum dedicated to lawnmowers, the only one in the world.

The British Lawnmower Museum is prominently flagged up in road signs as you enter to town, but rather tucked away in a labyrinth of side streets a short distance from the town centre. It attracts more than 6000 visitors a year, some of whom visit out of curiosity attracted by the quirky nature of the museum, others for a chance to connect to a bygone age.

The museum is the brainchild of Brian Radam who has spent a lifetime of involvement in the mower business. His father had opened Southport's first DIY shop in 1945 after the family's original shop in Liverpool was bombed during the war. The shop specialised in the repair of locks, safes and lawnmowers, and at the age of 10, Brian was helping out with the regrinding of lawnmower blades.

Leaving the family shop, he joined the famous Atco Lawnmower Company as an apprentice, helping with

Brian Radam

the repair and servicing of more 450 mowers a week, which were collected and delivered to customers by a team of Atco engineers using motorcycles and sidecars.

Brian also trained as Master Locksmith, and became a Fellow of the British Locksmiths Institute. The shop, in Shakespeare Street, Southport grew as a sales and repair centre for both locks and for lawnmowers.

Over the years, Brian had collected old mowers, mostly those that would otherwise have been scrapped but whose owners hated to see consigned to the rubbish tip. Most were fine examples of British engineering, but as the era of inexpensive electric mowers grew so popularity of heavy, petrol powered lawnmowers waned.

Buddings original patent document

Budding machine manufactured by Brian Radam

At one stage Brian had amassed over 1000 machines, but as he started to restore them, he decided that if there was declining market, then he should put them on show as a reminder of a golden age of mowing machines.

In 1988, he turned over the top floor of the shop to a display space and the British Lawnmower Museum was born. Initially there were something like 200 restored mowers on show, today there are almost 500, spanning 180 years of lawnmower production.

In recent times, the museum has expanded even more. The lawnmower shop has moved next door, allowing the exhibits to extend over three floors whilst allowing the lock and key business to still run side-by-side with the museum.

Brian Radam is a realist. He knows that you cannot turn the clock back, but that doesn't stop him wishing to remind us of times when British engineers ruled supreme. "Up to the Fifties" he says "Britain made the finest cars, the finest motorcycles and the finest lawnmowers. So I am saving their fine workmanship from the scrapheap and displaying it to the world with pride"

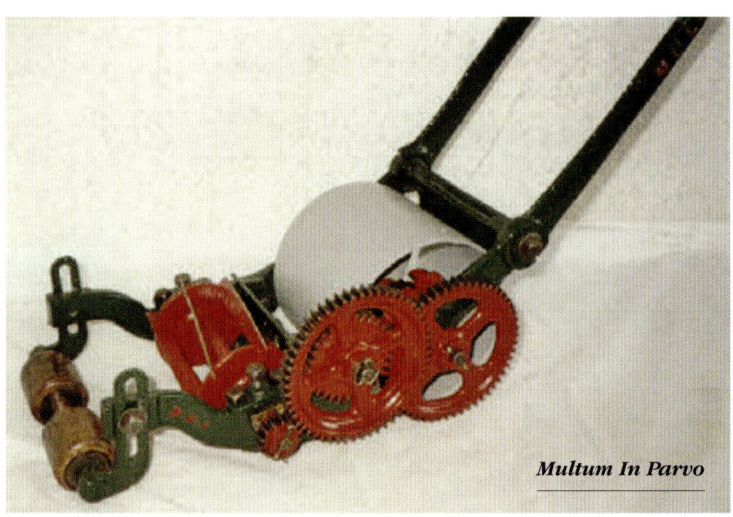

Multum In Parvo

A TREASURE TROVE

Anyone interested in engineering, in the progress of mechanisation or indeed in the social history of our land, will find plenty to engage and interest them. Naturally, pride of place as you step through the door, is the original Budding mower. The machine that started it all, looking remarkably similar to the many mowers that followed over the next century and a half.

Sadly, it is not an original. Of the 600 odd made by Budding in the 1830s, very few survived. There are perhaps five or six around today. One is in the possession of Ransomes, another in the Science Museum, one in the Stroud Museum and another at Reading University.

However, Brian Radam is the proud owner of a book of original patents which contains all the drawings used by Budding to obtain his lawnmower patent in 1830. Using the exact dimensions, a team of four skilled engineers spent 200 hours making a working replica of Budding's machine which was put through its paces by Brian who was a guest of engineer and TV presenter, Guy Martin, for his Channel Four series *How Britain Works*.

The somewhat clumbersome machine, it

Albert Pierpoint's mower

weighs a hefty 176lb (80kg), would be hard for many people to push (and pull), these days but the programme showed that it performed its primary function of cutting grass extremely efficiently.

"It proves that Edwin Budding was not only a talented inventor, but also a skilled engineer" says Brian "Remember he was doing everything from scratch. He had no similar designs to copy, no benchmark for a machine that could cut grass. It was remarkable achievement"

Brian went on to build four more 'Budding Original' replicas, which are now in the hands of private collectors.

Sitting alongside the Budding are a set of early horse-drawn mowers, and a huge push mower "the biggest in the world" says Brian, which again was specially made for a travelling puppet show.

As you look down the rows of shelves, stacked with mowers from every era, you get a sense evolution rather than revolution when it comes to the development of lawnmowers. There are some exquisite machines, including

The British Lawnmower Museum

one of Brian Radam's personal favourites, the Multum in Parvo mower with a 6" cutting cylinder made during the 1850s by Greens of Leeds.

Multum In Parvo is one of the strangest names ever given to a lawn mower and translated from the Latin means "much from little". Green's had already used a Latin name for its earlier Silens Messor model (Silent Running). The Multum In Parvo was a great success and many thousands were sold up to the 1930s when it was replaced.

Alongside the roll-call of mowers through the ages, are

Special Limited Edition Qualcast Concorde to mark 6 million machines

a number of machines that have been owned by well-known people. There's an Atco lawn tractor presented to the Prince of Wales and Princess Diana at the time of their wedding, a mower owned by Southport resident Jean Alexander (Hilda Ogden in Coronation Street) and rather bizarrely a 10" JP push mower owned by Britain's most

Black and Decker 'Drill' mower

famous hangman, Albert Pierpoint who retired to Southport before his death in 1992. Pierpoint hanged 400 people and received the sum of £15 for each hanging – co-incidentally the same price as the mower when new.

HOVER OR BOVVER?

Today many households have replaced mowers with petrol engines or indeed their push mowers with lightweight electric mowers, and indeed in the British Lawnmower Museum are examples of the early Flymo machines which took the country by storm as the first to use the hovercraft principle. With an electric mower, you plug in and mow, the only limitation being the length of the cable you need to stretch to the nearest power point. Mass production meant the price plummeted compared with many push or petrol mowers and 'the light main electrics' as they were called, soon dominated the market.

Early Flymo's are on show accompanied by their TV slogan made famous in the 1980's "It's a lot less bovver with hover". That phrase was later usurped by rivals Qualcast

First electric mower by Ransomes

Early Atco 21" mower

The Ransomes Electra was the UK's first commercially available electric powered mower. Other companies had tested electric powered mowers before this, and at least one manufacturer in the US began production of electric powered machines at around the same time, but the Electra was the first to be sold successfully in the UK. (pic 015)

Although mains power had been available for some time in the UK it was largely confined to towns and cities. Supply in rural areas was patchy at best although some larger houses were occasionally connected and a few even had their own generating plants.

To see how electric lawnmowers had progressed from crude beginnings, Brian shows off an early variation of a Black & Decker mower which uses a power drill to drive the blade, which can then be switched to using other tools such as a hedgetrimmer. A multi-purpose devise from the 1960's which unsurprisingly never really caught on!

The early 20th century saw the emergence of many specialist mower manufacturers, all aiming for a slice of the growing market. Companies such as JP, Greens, Folbate, Wilkinson Sword, Royal Enfield, British Anzani all flourished for a while but their names have disappeared, whilst others from that early era such as Dennis and Lloyds are still making specialist mowers for the sportsturf market.

Ransomes Ajax handmower

to promote their best selling Concorde electric cylinder mower. They changed their advertising subtly to read "It's a lot less bovver than a hover" It must have worked because the Concorde became the best selling mower of its age, and Brian has a special gold Concorde on show to commemorate the 6 millionth machine made.

So it was something of an anomaly to see the mower that Brian Radam views as one of his most important acquisitions. It is the first electric mower made by Ransomes in 1926. "That was a really groundbreaking development then, perhaps only matched by the new robotic mowers of today. Remember, this was a time when many people didn't even have electricity"

ATCO AND RANSOMES

Two brands however dominate much of the space at the museum. Atco and Ransomes. Atco are credited with making the first mass produced petrol lawnmower, the Atco Standard first manufactured in 1921 whilst Ransomes gave up their long agricultural heritage in the 1980s to focus entirely on the phenomenal success of its mower and grass machinery range.

Over the years, Ransomes mowers ('The Best in the World' ran their advertising) were known for their quality of engineering and quality of cut. That was especially true of their hand mowers, such as the Ransomes Ajax and fine cut Certes (although some developments like the odd shaped Conquest was not one of their finest moments)

A renovated Ransomes Ajax from the 1960s is still a sought-after machine. Costing £11.19s.6d, (equivalent to around £148 today). A refurbished machine today can sell of upwards of £350, and says Brian "They will be as good as new, will last a lifetime and produce a fine lawn, whilst giving the owner a very nice work-out'.

What you see at the British Lawnmower Museum is only the tip of the iceberg as far as Brian Radam's stock of mowers is concerned. In two sizeable nearby warehouses, he has rows and rows of old mowers just awaiting TLC. It is not that Brian is a hoarder (well not much), he recognises the work, skill and expertise that has gone into making these machines – and cannot bear to see them consigned to scrap metal. "They come to me because they are too old, too expensive to repair or parts are not available. Some we restore, and from others we can often supply parts that are no longer available, whilst some will find a place in the museum".

The British Lawnmower Museum is the only one of its kind in the world. It is often listed in newspaper features citing the Top Ten Oddball/Bizarre/Wierd Museums alongside the likes of the Pencil Museum, Bagpipe Museum and even the Dog Collar Museum.

However, 6000 visitors a year can't be wrong, and besides over 1 million mowers a year are sold in the UK, so it is hardly a minority interest. What is equally true is that many of the sceptics and those prepared to be bored are soon hooked by the sheer scale of the historical display.

Edwin Budding would surely be proud and honoured that his invention, his vision, and his legacy is recognised with flair and imagination after all these years in this dedicated homage to his long-lasting achievement.

Brian Radam's overflow stock of historic mowers

The British Lawnmower Museum

The Collectors

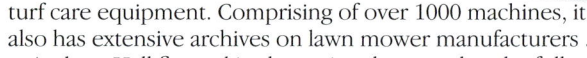

One of the UK's largest lawnmower collections, The Hall & Duck Trust, was established in 1982. Andrew Hall and Mike Duck, well known lawn mower collectors, were commissioned by Ransomes for their exhibition celebrating 150 years of lawn mower manufacture to stage an exhibition of vintage mowers.

Today the Hall & Duck Trust is an internationally recognised organisation, preserving all manner of artefacts from lawn mower development throughout the years and is also a respected authority on the history of the lawn-mower.

The Hall & Duck Trust collections house lawn mowers from the 1830s to the 1940s and also includes other period turf care equipment. Comprising of over 1000 machines, it also has extensive archives on lawn mower manufacturers.

Andrew Hall figured in the national press when he fully restored one of the world's first motorised lawnmowers to its former glory, spending four years working on the 1.25 ton machine.

The Ransomes mower cost £137 in 1902, equivalent to £15,000 today. It was initially purchased by Cadbury's and used in the Bournville village in Warwickshire to maintain a sports field. It was then bought second-hand by Peugeot Talbot in 1923 to mow their sports field in Coventry. However, when the firm extended their pavilion they built a new structure over the top of the machine, totally encasing it.

There, it lay forgotten for more than 50 years until the building was demolished. Mower enthusiast Mr Hall was then given the machine which he has painstakingly restored.

"When I first saw the mower it looked a bit forlorn, but after I was given it I realised it was the first one that Ransomes made when I spotted the identification number"

'It has taken four years to restore it and I would say it was 60 per cent intact, but I had to build some new parts. It runs a bit slower than a modern lawn mower, but when the engine is running everybody knows about it because it is like a traction engine"

Budding's Legacy Series

Iconic lawnmowers that have shaped the industry

NUMBER 4: JP Mowers

Leicester based engineers Jerram and Pearson (JP) set out to make the best lawnmowers in the world in the Twenties. The JP Super one of the most popular and successful hand mowers of the 1920s and 1930s. They were also very expensive, even for those days.

During the same period, the company also manufactured motor mowers. These machines were produced to the same high quality standards for which JP was best known. In fact, the company's own sales brochures referred to them as the "Rolls Royce of Lawn Mowers" (fitting because Rolls Royce was to later buy the company)

The most interesting and unusual mower was the 24" JP Super Power Mower which featured a water cooled four stroke engine with an open topped water hopper that resembles a small cauldron or cooking pot!

The mower was designed so that the entire engine unit could be removed easily for maintenance and repair. The cutting cylinder was also easily removed by simply undoing a couple of retainers and lifting it out.

Another of the design features that made the 24" JP Super Power Mower unusual in its time was the starting mechanism. This was an early type of rope or pull start, whereas during the same period most motor mowers featured crank handle starting. JP claimed this made the mower easier to start and, to illustrate the point, showed the mower being started by a young woman in some of its advertisements.

JP became a victim of the Rolls Royce collapse of 1971 as they had been a major supplier of machined components to them. The company was bought from the receivers by Howardson, manufacturers of Dennis Mowers in 1990 and many of the features introduced by JP were incorporated in the Dennis mower range.

Ready, Steady, Mow!

In 1991, one of Great Britain's finest ever relay squad stormed to victory in the 4 x 400m relay final at the World Championships held in Tokyo. They beat the mighty US reigning world champions, who were anchored by the newly crowned 400m king Antonio Pettigrew.

The GB team were Roger Black, Derek Redmond, John Regis and Kris Akabusi It was a performance that saw the team included in the Greatest Team in the History of Sport shortlist published by US broadcaster ESPN.

In 2015, to mark the introduction InStart, a new push button starting system for lawnmowers, engine maker Briggs & Stratton reunited the team for the first time in 24 years. Swapping their batons for mowers, they took part in a Lawnmower Race under the watchful eye of racing driver and motoring journalist, Tiff Needell

Budding's Legacy Series

Iconic lawnmowers that have shaped the industry

NUMBER 5: Atco Mowers

Atco is one of the most famous names in British lawn mower history. In 1921 Charles H Pugh Ltd started making motor mowers under the trade name Atco (short for "Atlas Chain Company").

The Atco Standard and was an immediate success. 900 of them were made in 1921, each costing £75. Within five years, annual production had accelerated to tens of thousands. Prices were cut and a range of sizes was available, making the Atco Standard the first truly mass-produced motor mower.

The company was highly successful throughout the decades that followed, especially in producing quality, value for money machines for the domestic market and cost effective larger machines for professional use.

Atco always excelled in the simplicity of design. The early motor mowers pioneered the idea of mass production in the new mower manufacturing industry. Designing complete ranges of mowers around near-identical components, the company was able to simplify construction and service/support so that reduced costs could be passed on to customers. The formula was a great success, and the concept was still evident in the 1960s and beyond.

Mowers of this period still had the 'classic' Atco features: simple side-frames forming a chassis to support the mid-mounted engine; the familiar petrol tank mounted on

Preparing for the Open at St. Andrews

the handlebars; the large capacity grass box.

In the 1960s, the range extended from 12in to 34in models. The 28in and 34in models were almost identical, and both were available with trailed seat to allow the gardener to ride behind the machine, essential for jobs that involved cutting large expanses of grass.

Atco continued making mowers at Derby until a fire destroyed its factory in 1981 when production moved to Stowmarket in Suffolk. In 1991, the company became Atco-Qualcast and was acquired by Bosch in 1995.

In 2011, Bosch sold the tooling, drawings and manufacturing rights to Allett Ltd, but the Atco brand name was bought by Global Garden Products group based in Italy but with a subsidiary in Plymouth from where an Atco brand range are sold alongside its other brands of Mountfield and Stiga.

WIMBLEDON
Turf perfection

IF Edwin Budding was to look down today to assess the impact of his invention more than 180 years earlier - and he had the benefit of something like Google Earth - there is little doubt that he would zoom in on a collection of grass rectangles to the south west of London.

The All England Lawn Tennis Club at Wimbledon is perhaps the embodiment of his achievement. The annual Championships are regarded as one of the world's leading sporting events, as much for the facilities, presentation and socialising, as for the standard of tennis played during the two week tournament.

To win the US, French or Australian Open are special achievements, but to be crowned Wimbledon Champion has been the pinnacle for tennis players throughout the ages.

And what makes Wimbledon unique and special of course, is that it is the only major tennis championship to be played on grass in the world.

Whilst other sports dally with the introduction of non-grass or artificial surfaces, you will find no such talk at the All England Lawn Tennis Club. Grass, stripes, strawberries and cream are all an essential element of the Wimbledon DNA – and highly unlikely to ever change.

Leading players of every era agree. The celebrated Australian great, Rod Laver, winner of four Wimbledon Singles Championships, says "The game is still best when it is played, as it was originally, on grass"

FIRST CHAMPIONSHIP

There is little doubt that the origins of Wimbledon, and indeed of lawn tennis itself, were influenced by two key inventions in the early part of the 19th century. First, of course Budding's lawnmower in 1830 and ten years later the invention of vulcanised rubber which made possible the bouncing tennis ball.

The All England Croquet Club was formed in 1868 by six gentlemen who then set about finding a venue for their new club. After a year-long search they decided upon a four acres site between the South Western Railway and Worple Road in Wimbledon, an outer suburb of London.

However, the waning popularity of croquet, coupled with increasing interest and participation in lawn tennis, resulted in the installation of four tennis courts by 1875 and a name change to the All England Croquet and Lawn Club.

This coincided with the rules of lawn tennis being finalised by the Marylebone Cricket Club (MCC) who adapted them from the game of real tennis in 1875.

The first Gentlemen's Singles championship was played on a grass court at Wimbledon in June 1877. There were just 22 competitors and the tournament was watched by around 200 spectators. The final was won in 48 minutes by Spencer Gore, a 27-year old rackets player from Wandsworth who defeated William Marshall to win the first prize of 12 guineas and a silver challenge cup. It was reported that tournament made a £10 profit.

Tennis had been included in the Olympic Games since 1896, and with the 1908 Games being staged in London, the tennis tournament was played both indoors (at Queens Club) and outdoors at Wimbledon. The Men's singles was won by Josiah Ritchie of Great Britain, whist Dorothea Lambert Chambers, also Great Britain, won the Women's Singles.

Tennis was then excluded from the Olympics from 1924, only returning to the schedule in 1988.

The 2012 London Olympics were an opportunity for a return to Wimbledon and to the delight of the home fans, the Mens Singles Gold Medal was won by Andy Murray, with the Women's Gold going to Serena Williams.

NINE ACRES OF FINE GRASS

Today, the Wimbledon Championships are played out in front of a capacity crowd of more than 490,000 over the two weeks and a global TV audience estimated at over 378 million globally.

All of which places enormous pressure on those responsible for staging the Championships, and not least head groundsman, Neil Stubley and his team of 16 full time grounds staff, a total which rises to 28 in the run up to the Championships.

Neil joined the Wimbledon groundstaff in 1995 after studying turf care at college. "It's all I ever wanted to do" he says. He worked his way up through the grounds team, and took over the lead role from Eddie Seaward, the man the *New York Times* once called *Wimbledon's Wizard of the Lawn*, who retired as Head Groundsman in 2012.

There are 41 grass courts that make up the Wimbledon

tennis complex, of which 19 are tournament courts (there is no Court 13) and 22 practice courts. Then of course there are the extensive grass areas that need to be kept neat and tidy.

With each court and surrounds measuring 41 metres by 22 metres (902 sq metres) that's almost 37,000 sq metres of fine grass to prepare and maintain – or just over 9 acres in total.

All of which means an extensive range of machinery. 26 cylinder mowers, 4 rotary mowers, triple mowers, ride-on mowers – and even a robotic mower for hillsides and banks too steep for an operator to mow safely.

Naturally, all 41 courts, both matchplay and practice, have to be of the same consistent quality. Mown to perfection, perfectly striped and with a durability to cope with the 700-odd matches, and hours of practice during the Championship

Work starts on court preparation for the following year immediately the Championships have finished. It's a

complex programme of logistics and timing for Neil and his grounds team. The All England Lawn Tennis Club is still exactly that, a membership tennis club. Members can use the courts, other than the show courts (Centre and Number One) during the Club season which runs from the beginning of May to the end of September, except for a week before the Championships begin, and for 36 hours after they finish.

First task for the renovation of each court is 'fraise mowing', a process that strips out the old and worn grass before re-seeding can take place. The work continues during the Autumn and into the Winter when the grass is then cut every week if weather conditions permit and left at healthy 13mm in length.

In the Spring, the work intensifies. The courts are cut at least three times a week, then every day during the Championships, with the height of cut lowered to the optimum length of 8mm.

The amount of work that the mowers have to undertake means constant servicing and repairs when necessary, so Neil has a well-equipped service workshop on site staffed by two full time mechanics.

The installation of a retractable roof on Centre Court a few years ago has actually increased the essential sunlight needed for the healthy growth of grass, and can be closed to undertake essential renovation work if required "But has rarely been needed" says Neil.

OLYMPIAN PERFORMANCE

The usual court renovation programme can be disrupted if extra major tournaments are added such as Davis Cup tie – and more recently the Olympics tennis tournament in 2012.

A Davis Cup tie will only use one show court, whilst the Olympics utilised 10 tournament courts, plus practice facilities, and was to provide the biggest challenge that Neil Stubley and his team would ever face. It was to be a huge challenge for the new and old guard, with Neil taking over from Eddie Seaward at the end of the summer – and it needed the experience and 'nouse' of both men to achieve a dauntingly quick turnaround between the Championships and the Olympics.

The timescale was straightforward. The 2012 Wimbledon Championship ran between 25th June and 8th July. It then became a race against time to renovate the match courts back to their pristine state in just 20 days before the scheduled first matches in the Olympics on 28th July.

"As with every year, most of the wear to the court takes place on the base lines and through the centre of the court" says Neil "so for two years, Eddie and I in conjunction with the Sports Turf Research Institute (STRI) in Yorkshire had been trialling different types of grass seeds that would be fast growing and hard wearing"

These were then pre-germinated ahead of the Olympics in special trays, so no time was wasted in applying the seed to the used courts. Planning was the key, smoothing out the potential pitfalls, and factoring in the unknown - such as the weather which was extremely wet in the run up to the Games.

In the event, the courts looked fantastic, played immaculately, and the transformation was accomplished. It was a triumph for science - and for people. Preparing and maintaining the courts at Wimbledon is daunting and exhausting work for Neil and his team. To do it all over again so soon was an incredible feat – and unlike anything else faced by groundstaff during Wimbledon's long history. Their efforts deservedly won the Team of the Year Award in 2012 presented by leading turf magazine, Turf Pro.

"We are privileged to work on the best grass in the world" says Neil "Compared with any other country, it looks different - and it smells different "

Despite his enhanced responsibilities as Head Groundsman at one of the most famous sporting venues in the world, Neil still enjoys getting out in the fresh air with a mower in hand. "I can think of nothing more therapeutic or relaxing" he says "it allows you space to think, the hum of the mower, the satisfaction of a fine cut, straight lines, light and shade. Perfection!"

What music that would have been to Edwin Budding's ears, to hear such appreciation of his invention from all those years ago.

Where the action is
Turf professionals have a unique opportunity to be part of the world's greatest sporting events

What would any young person give to have a close-up view of Wimbledon fortnight, be on the golf course for a Ryder Cup match-up or pitchside at the world's most famous football fixture, El Clasico when Real Madrid take on Barcelona?

Being a groundsman is often regarded by career advisors as a fall-back job for those lacking in academic skills or not of university standard. Indeed, the public perception tends to be of someone in wellies, wielding a fork and painting white lines. Nothing could be further from the truth, the opportunities for those willing to work hard, become part of a team and learn are immense.

Take three young men, who decided to follow their dream. They probably did not start out with stars in their eyes. They wanted a satisfying job, one that might open up opportunities, one in which they had to the chance to learn on the job.

Neil Stubley, *(below)* today holds the key position of Head Groundsman at the All England Lawn Tennis Club, home to the prestigious Wimbledon Championships. He had enrolled in the Norwood Hall Institute of Horticultural Education in West London (now closed) straight from school, and afterwards joined the groundstaff at Wimbledon.

Scott Fenwick, born in Dundee, raised in Perth, joined the greenkeeping staff at Gleneagles straight from school. Today, Scott is Golf Courses and Estate Manager at the famous Perthshire hotel and golf resort which has not only hosted two G8 Summits for world leaders but became the focus of worldwide interest when it hosted the 2014 Ryder Cup, watched by millions around the world

At the age of 14, **Paul Burgess**, read an article about the day-to-day job of the Arsenal head groundsman and decided that was to be his career. Starting at Blackpool FC, he got the opportunity to join the Arsenal groundstaff, working first at Highbury then at the newly built Emirates Stadium. In 2009, he was approached by Real Madrid and today is Head Groundsman for the famous La Liga club, responsible for the pitch at the 81,000 capacity Bernabeu Stadium and training facilities

All three have reached the top of their chosen profession. All took learning opportunities and sat exams to improve their qualifications along the way, but probably none of them would have had their present status in mind when they left school.

SCIENTIST – AND DIPLOMAT

Make no mistake, the groundsman of today has to be many, many things. Agronomist, scientist, grafter, optimist, weather-expert, technician, man-manager – and diplomat.

There is a saying that a good pitch, a good playing surface, should be like a good referee. Integral to the play and complimentary to the skills of the players – but not be noticed.

When a referee (or umpire) is having a bad day, he becomes the story. It's the same with the pitch.

When great chunks of turf come off the surface, everybody notices. When a cricket pitch goes bad (as happened in Jamaica in 1998 when a Test Match was abandoned) it becomes the story. When a golfer missed a putt, then it's the fault of the greens! The Wembley pitch, rather than the stadium itself became the story after the rebuild. The Millenium Stadium struggled to present a consistent surface for many years after the rebuild from the old Cardiff Arms Park

Neil Stubley found himself at the centre of controversy in 2013 when on a single day early in the Championships a record number of seven players either withdrew in mid-match due to injuries, or handed a walkover to their opponents. Many laid the blame on a 'slippery court'.

Scott Fenwick

It became a major media story for several days, with Stubley, supported by the All England Club, issuing a statement that "The courts have been prepared in exactly the same way as in previous years, the grass is the same, the soil is the same and our height of cut is the same" He added "Our stats are showing the courts are playing exactly as they have been in previous years".

Diplomatically, Neil Stubley will say that player feedback is important and vital to the continual improvement of the courts. He adds that todays players are acutely knowledgeable about court preparation. "They don't leave anything to chance. Just like their diet is controlled, the time they eat and drink is controlled, so they want to know when the court was cut before their match and any information they can lay their hands on to feed into their personal 'stats-bank'"

"However, with Wimbledon being the only major Championship played on grass, they will realise that the surface is very different to hard or clay court courts elsewhere. Grass is a living, breathing, wearing plant which throws up a whole new set of playing characteristics".

For Scott Fenwick, the Ryder Cup was always going to be the highlight of his long career at Gleneagles which has three courses, the PGA Centenary Course (formerly the Monarch course) which hosted the Ryder Cup, the Kings Course and Queens Course.

This was to be the first Ryder Cup to be staged in Scotland since the 1973 match. Gleneagles was awarded the event in 2001 and had more than ten years to prepare the venue.

Designed by Jack Nicklaus and opened in 1993, the PGA Centenary Course was extensively re-modelled by Nicklaus in the run-up to the 2014 Ryder Cup.

Working with Centenary course manager, Steve Chappell, Fenwick planned an almost military-style operation to ensure that nothing was left to chance. However, this being Scotland in late September, the weather could always have been a factor. The previous two Ryder Cups on this side of the Atlantic, at The K Club Dublin in 2006 then Celtic Manor in 2010, were both hit by bad weather. "All you can do is prepare for every eventuality," he says.

Ryder Cup captain Paul McGinley visited the course several times after been appointed captain of the European team. He worked closely with Scott, Steve and the greenkeeping team to prepare the course exactly how he wanted it for his players.

"For instance, he took in account the big hitting prowess of players like Bubba Watson and Dustin Johnson to influence how long the rough should be" said Steve Chappell.

The roll on the green is measured precisely with a stimp-meter. On an average day the greenkeepers aim for a green speed of around 10 feet but this goes up to 11 feet for tournaments. In the same way that Neil Stubley's preparation at Wimbledon has to be the same for each and every court, Scott says that "the most important consideration for leading golf professionals is that all 18 greens are consistent".

For the event, the 26 strong Gleneagles greenkeeping staff was bolstered the arrival of more than 50 experienced greenkeepers from the UK and around the world – such is attraction and 'kudos' of the chance to be part of one of the greatest sports shows on earth.

The European team won a resounding victory, defeating the US for the third time in a row. The players celebrated in style, as did the greenkeeping team who had contribute so much to the event.

Business being business, and Gleneagles is business first and foremost. With all the structures, stands, hospitality units, TV towers, broadcasting studios still in place (they wouldn't be fully removed until November), the course had to be got ready to host playing guests by 10.00am on the Monday morning following the final day on Sunday.

"We used a white line to find out which of the greenkeeping team could walk the straightest the following morning, in order to send a couple of them out to cut the greens!" said Steve Chappell.

Paul Burgess at The Bernabeu

BLACKPOOL TO THE BERNABEU

Paul Burgess was prompted to try his hand at being a groundsman after reading that article about Arsenal's head groundsman, Steve Braddock, whilst still at school

He got a job as an Apprentice Groundsman with Blackpool FC at Bloomfield Road, and studied turfcare at Lancashire's Myerscough College. Spotting an advertisement for an Assistant Groundsman for Arsenal at the old Highbury ground, he got the job and in 2000 moved to London. Although still in his 20s, Paul was promoted to Head Groundman, when Steve Braddock moved to look

Paul Burgess at The Emirates

after the state-of-the-art Arsenal training facilities.

Arsenal manager, Arsene Wenger has always been an advocate of having the finest playing surface possible to compliment the skills of his players, so when the Club's new Emirates Stadium was being constructed, Paul was fully involved in the design process along with the Club Management Team and the Stadium architects to ensure that optimum light and airflow was available to allow the grass to prosper.

After 12 years' service at Arsenal, where he received numerous awards for making the pitches at Highbury and the Emirates standard-setters across the world, the 32-year old took a call asking him to move to Madrid and rescue the turf at the Santiago Bernabeu stadium. "The call from Real Madrid was a bit out of the blue! I'd been at Arsenal for 12 years and I wasn't actively looking to go somewhere else but I was certainly ready for a new challenge." he says

"I think quite a few players got injuries on the pitch and they just ran out of patience, so rather than just chucking money at re-turfing it they looked around for what they thought was the best pitch and it went from there,"

Burgess is facing different challenges in Madrid. "The 70m-high stands restrict the amount of sunlight the pitch receives, and the vast range in Madrid's temperatures means that growing grass in the city is a 'disaster'".

"There is a different kind of pressure compare with Arsenal" he says "Real Madrid is all about today. If they don't do well today there is no tomorrow, winning is everything"

"That transcends down to the groundsman. Everyone at the club has to have a winning mentality and if you don't have that, then you aren't part of the make-up of the club."

Paul is still amazed at his progress to the top "I didn't think reading that article back then that one day I would ever be here at the Bernabeu. I remember going to see Real Madrid against Barcelona a few years ago when David Beckham scored and I said to my girlfriend I'd love to work here".

"Even now when I walk into the Bernabeu it gives you a special feeling - one you don't get in other stadiums".

So what next, is there anywhere else he would consider working after Real Madrid?

"If Blackpool ever get into the Champions League then I've said I would go back there!" he says.

Millennium Stadium, Cardiff

WANT TO KNOW MORE?

If you are interested to learn more about a career in groundsmanship or greenkeeping, you can get plenty of information from two trade associations regarding job opportunities, training and qualifications.

Institute of Groundsmanship (IOG)
28 Stratford Office Village
Walker Avenue
Wolverton Mill East
Milton Keynes
Bucks MK12 5TW
Tel: 01908 312511
www.iog.org

British and International Golf Greenkeepers Association (BIGGA)
BIGGA House
Aldwark Alne
York YO61 1UK
Tel: 01347 833800
www.bigga.org.uk

Pitching in
Looking after cricket's headquarters, except when archery takes over

Mick Hunt started at Lords in 1969 as a junior groundsman and worked his way up the ladder. "Lords is special" he say "and with its quirks like the slope of the pitch and the sheer number of matches that take place here compared to at other grounds. Every year Lord's hosts two Tests, one day internationals, club finals, domestic finals, village finals. There are six full-time members on the groundstaff and from April to the first week of October we work seven days a week and 10,11, 12 hour days"

'The job changes all the time. The pressure's increased and there's greater expectation both from players and

Olympic archery at Lords 2012

the public. My main priority is preparing the square. We spend a lot of time looking upwards to the sky. I've got a computerised irrigation system for when it gets too dry, and mechanised 'blotters' to cope with down pours"

'After each match, the umpire marks the pitch on a scale of one to six – very good, good, average, below average, poor and unfit – and we're always in the top category, so we're doing our bit. I don't get to watch much cricket because when there's a match on we usually work on the adjoining Nursery (training) ground.

'We see a lot of wildlife here: kestrels and sparrowhawks, plus the odd racing pigeon. We found a peacock strutting about here a few years ago'. We also have a lot of foxes. They've become a real nuisance. Over the past the past two winters we must have caught in the region of fifty per winter.

'I enjoy my job. But on Test match mornings I'll be sick with worry. I know a couple of ex-professional cricketers who've become groundsmen and say the job's ten times more stressful than playing cricket because of the expectations. We've had occasions where the pitch has been superb but team A has been far superior than team B and it has been one sided, but it still doesn't stop people saying "What's wrong with the pitch!".

'But, being truthful, before a Test match when the ground just looks superb, I get a real buzz. I get a buzz in September when it's all over as well!'

RACE AGAINST TIME

Normally, Lords is only used for cricket, no pop concerts, rugby in the winter. But in 2012, Mick Hunt had to hand over his 'kingdom' for several weeks in the middle of the cricket season to the 2102 Olympic authority for the Home of Cricket was selected as the venue for the Olympic archery competition.

As well as the archers and targets, special temporary stands were set up on the outfield to bring spectators closer to the action. It would have also been one of the very few times that a South Korean and a Mexican would have walked down the steps of the famous old pavilion.

Throughout the entire Olympic period, Mick Hunt and his staff continued to maintain the square and to prepare the Test pitch – except during the actual competition of course! The archers aimed across the roped off cricket square to the target during the competition, although the odd stray arrow did embed itself in the hallowed turf. But then Lord's had just under two weeks to get its outfield up to scratch for the Test match between England and South Africa. During that 13 day window, all the stands had to be dismantled, still leaving Mick and his team room to prepare for one of the most important Test Matches in the cricketing calendar.

Some areas of the outfield had to be returfed, but the venue looked spick and span to the thousands of cricket followers who turned up for the Test Match.

Mick won the Cricket Groundsman of the Year Award in 2012, and for the special match staged at Lords in 2014 between the MCC and a Rest of the World XI to mark the MCC's Bicentenary, he was invited to ring the bell to signify the start of play.

Budding's Legacy Series

Iconic lawnmowers that have shaped the industry

NUMBER 6: Hayter Hayterette

The Hayterette petrol lawnmower was launched in the 1970s by Hayter. Designed and built at the company's factory near Bishops Stortford, Hertforshire, the model has been in production for over fifty years – and is still a popular best seller.

The Hayterette became the workhorse of the Hayter range, strong, reliable, used by contractors and homeowners alike.

In many ways, the Hayterette is a no-frills grass cutter. It has no grass collector, a very shallow deck and was designed for maintaining rough grassed areas.

It is manufactured with a cast aluminium deck rather than the more common pressed steel and has reinforced axle plates for reliability.

The blade arrangement is unusual, four swinging  blades are mounted on a rotating disc which helps protect the crankshaft from damage in the more challenging terrain it is designed for. However, this did not prevent the Hayterette being portrayed as machine ideal for the lady of the house to use, often set in a lifestyle setting

These days the Hayter Hayterette is fitted with a Briggs & Stratton four stroke petrol engine and sells for over £600.

Lions and the Lawn
Greening of Trafalgar Square Heritage

Dominated by the huge column that celebrates Lord Nelson, Britain's greatest military hero, **Trafalgar Square** is at the heart of the capital, and is on countless occasions the heartbeat of the nation.

Surrounded by Victorian architecture such as the magnificent National Gallery, the square is no relic of a bygone age. Instead of statues of military heroes, the celebrated Fourth Plinth is used for exciting and controversial modern art. Free outdoor events are held in summer, the famous Oslo Christmas Tree dominated in the winter, and it is the traditional end point for protest marches and a rallying point for British counter-culture.

It was in the Trafalgar Square that London's successful bid for the 2012 Olympics was celebrated, and it's granite surface plays host to a variety of events during the year.

But on a least two occasions, the square has been given a much softer look with the addition of fine turf.

In 2005, a special grass tennis court was built to host a special match between Boris Becker and Tim Henman as part of a nationwide search to find the future stars of British tennis.

The special reinforced turf grown with a hardwearing tennis mixture was grown by Lindum Turf at their turf fields in York. It has been mown and fertilised to provide good ball bounce and was lifted the previous evening, arriving onsite at Trafalgar Square at midnight the night before the match. With just eight hours to go, contractors prepared a drainage system and began the long and delicate job of laying the turf.

The final preparations including mowing and linemarking were completed and the netting was set up moments before the events was due to start.

At the conclusion, the grass tennis court disappeared as quickly as it had appeared, and Trafalgar Square was once again returned to its more usual stone-coloured complexion.

A TURF CARPET

In May 2007, Lindum Turf was again involved in a similar but much bigger project. As part of the London's Villages Campaign, organised by Visit London to promote the city, over 2000 square metres of specially grown turf was grown and transported to London overnight to cover virtually the whole of Trafalgar Square.

The green sward covered the entire flat area between the two fountains and around Nelson's Column giving visitors and city workers a green parkland environment.

Lindum's Stephen Fell, said the whole mood of the square had changed. "Covering it with grass, changed the atmosphere and encouraged people to stop, sit and picnic, much as they would in a London park."

After two days, the turf was lifted and transported to a permanent place alongside the Thames at Hammersmith. Once again Trafalgar Square was returned to normal – and the pigeons could stop wondering whether their normal feeding surface would ever be the same again!

Lions and the Lawn

PROFILE: MOWER MAKERS

Briggs and Stratton: The Legend

The power behind the World's Lawnmowers

Many owners of petrol powered lawnmowers believe that their machine is called a Briggs & Stratton - despite the fact that the company has never made or marketed a lawnmower under its own name.

However, the fact is that millions of lawnmowers over the years have been powered by Briggs & Stratton engines, so that the familiar red and black logo is often just as recognisable as the brand of mower to which it is fitted.

The Briggs & Stratton story dates back to 1908 when a college graduate Stephen F Briggs and grain company executive Harold M Stratton got together to manufacture and market a six cylinder, two stroke engine. It was a partnership in which Briggs was the inventor, Stratton the investor.

It was a project that never got off the ground, but they were hooked on the potential of the automotive market at a time when mass production made cars more affordable, thanks to the likes of Henry Ford and his early Model T.

Over the years, the young entrepeneurs dabbled in many markets including radios, washing machine engines, refrigerators, locks, ignition systems and small engines.

Eventually they settled on two solid and growing businesses, automotive locks and small engines, which the company started producing in 1920.

The big breakthrough came in the 1950s when Briggs & Stratton pioneered an aluminium alloy engine that was both lightweight and inexpensive. It was a time when the growing masses of Americans were migrating to the suburbs and the demand for lawnmowers and gardening equipment grew rapidly.

INNOVATION

Today, Briggs & Stratton manufactures around 10 million engines a year, making it the world's largest manufacturer of small engines for lawnmowers and power equipment, with 8 out of 10 mowers in the United States using a Briggs and Stratton engine.

With the protection of the environment a key concern today, Briggs & Stratton engines made today have 75% fewer emissions than those sold before 1995, and the company is committed to cutting energy use by 25% in the next 10 years.

Briggs & Stratton has always been at the forefront of innovation – and that is vividly illustrated by the company's latest development.

In a survey conducted at the Harrogate Flower Show in 2014, mower owners were asked what they didn't like

about their current mower. Of those who had an electric mower, 50% said they didn't like coping with the electric lead, whilst 33% of owners of a mower with a petrol engine were adamant – they didn't like the starting.

So for 2015, Briggs & Stratton have come up with a clever idea that combines the ease of an electric mower with the flexibility of a petrol mower. An engine which starts at the push of a button.

The Briggs and Stratton InStart system, which will be seen on more and more mower models from 2015 uses the latest in Lithium-Ion battery technology, which fits directly into the engine itself. So no more pull cord, no electric cable, just effortless starting.

The InStart battery will deliver over 50 starts on a single one-hour charge. Don't want to wait an hour? The rapid recharge feature provides up to 20 starts with only a 10-minute charge.

And another major 2015 development will see the introduction of a new range of Briggs & Stratton engines that will rarely need an oil change for the life of the lawnmower engine. All that is needed is to occasionally check the oil and add more when necessary, setting a new standard in ease of use.

Mr Briggs and Mr Stratton got together to innovate in 1908 – and today Briggs & Stratton is still loyal to their ideals.

Profile: Mower Makers

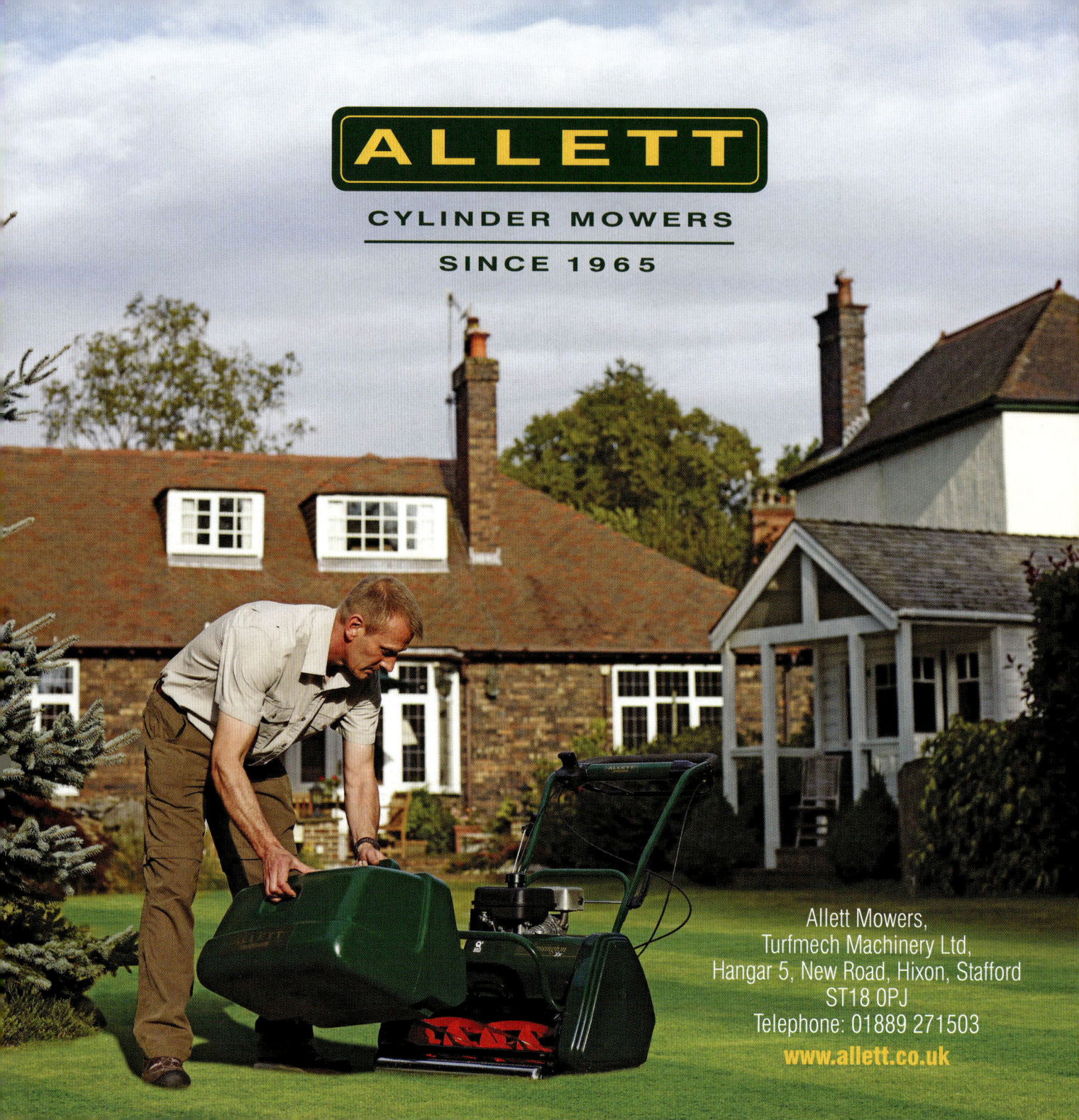

Budding's Legacy Series

Iconic lawnmowers that have shaped the industry

NUMBER 7: Suffolk Colt and Punch

In many respects the Suffolk Punch was the first 'modern' motor lawn mower.

When the Suffolk Punch was introduced in 1954 it represented more of an evolution than a revolution in mower design. The major components were made from pressed steel and light weight alloys when most of the machines from rival manufacturers were still being built with cast iron and heavy gauge sheet steel.

The Punch, made by Suffolk Iron Foundries of Stowmarket, was fitted with the company's own four-stroke engine in an era when most mowers had either Villiers or JAP engines.

The mower was named after the well known breed of 'Shire' horse, an equestrian theme continued with models introduced later in the 1950s and 1960s with names such as the Colt and Pony.

The Suffolk Colt was introduced in 1959 and went on to become one of the most popular motor mowers of the 1960s.

The design of the Suffolk Colt was very similar to the earlier Suffolk Punch although it was smaller and more compact. Both machines had a number of features in common, including almost identical versions of Suffolk's own 75cc four stroke engine. Suffolk was probably the last major UK lawn mower manufacturer to use its own engines and over two and a half million units were made by the company.

The Colt was available in 12" cutting width. It was a very compact design which made it ideal for smaller lawns in an era before electric power was available or accepted by the market.

Suffolk eventually became part of the Atco Qualcast group of companies, and mower production at Stowmarket ceased after the company was bought by Bosch, although Bosch today market their own brand of garden machinery in the UK.

Budding's Legacy Series

Iconic lawnmowers that have shaped the industry

NUMBER 8: BRITISH ANZANI

The British Anzani Easimow and its successor the Lawnrider are two of the most distinctive mowers of the past 50 years. When introduced in the early 1950s the Easimow was one of the first mowers specifically designed as a ride on machine for the domestic, as opposed to professional, market.

The Easimow was originally designed and manufactured by E F Ranger Ltd before manufacturing rights were acquired by British Anzani, an established and well-known manufacturer of agricultural and horticultural machinery. The company had links to the Anzani company the manufacturer of aeronautical and aircraft engines in the early years of the 20th century.

The Easimow was a very basic design. A tubular steel frame supported the engine and cutting assemblies as well as the roller seat. The mower was articulated in the middle and was steered using what might best be described as a cross between bicycle and pram handles. The early models had a 16" cut and were sold for £80.

In the early 1960s the Easimow was developed into the Lawnrider. This mower, available in 18" and 24" versions, had the same basic configuration but the major difference was that the chassis was now enclosed in sculpted steel panels.

Brian Radam on a British Anzani

An unusual feature of both the Easimow and the Lawnrider is that they are basically "front wheel drive". One of the innovations of the Lawnrider was that the cutting cylinder could be lifted from the lawn while the mower was in motion for easier travelling between tasks. This also enabled the Lawnrider to be used for other tasks around the garden in conjunction with attachments such as a trailer.

By the late 1960s British Anzani was facing stiffer competition and the company stopped making the Lawnrider. The company had disappeared from the market by the early 1970s.

Budding and Ransomes

More than 150 years of mower production

Early set of Ransomes gang mower

The Suffolk firm of Ransomes had already been in existence for over 40 years before Edwin Budding invented the lawnmower. In 1789, Robert Ransome started a foundry in Ipswich to make plough shares for the local farming community. A chance discovery of a method to make 'chilled' cast iron shares with extra hardness, which the company patented, resulted in demand from across the country and a significant lift in fortunes

Robert Ransome's, two sons joined the company in 1815, followed by his grandson James Allen Ransome in 1830. By this time, Ransomes was fully engaged in manufacturing ploughs, threshing machines and implements for agriculture.

There seems to have been no particular reason for the company to diversify, but James Allen was determined to make an impact on the business started by his grandfather, and when the opportunity to buy a manufacturing licence for Edwin Budding's new grass cutting machine cropped up, he grabbed it. It was perhaps a safeguard against the ups and down of the farm machinery business because this was a time of considerable unrest in the countryside as mechanisation took hold, resulting in major disturbances by distressed farm labourers.

In the following twenty years, the company then called J.R. & A Ransome only made 70 to 80 mowing machines each year – but they were exported across the world. To Government House in Calcutta, the Victoria Racecourse in Melbourne, for golf courses in Brazil and the West Indies. In 1896 came the breakthrough with the design of a petrol driven lawnmower, which Ransomes developed, patented and manufactured in 1902.

ABOVE: Ransomes Overgreen

GANG MOWER REVOLUTION

By the 1900s, Ransomes was a significant name in agriculture. Company representatives travelled the world gaining big orders – in 1908, 338 threshing machines were ordered for the Russian market. The new king, Edward V11 honoured Ransomes with a Royal Warrant – and ordered one of the company's new petrol-driven mowers for Buckingham Palace.

The 1914-1918 Great War meant a shift to the production of vehicles and munitions for the war effort and a temporary slowing of farm and grass machinery production.

With production was up and running again, new products were being constantly developed. One of the first innovations were gang mowers, first designed to be pulled by horses then by tractors.

The rage for golf in both Europe and the United States brought huge opportunity for Ransomes with the introduction of three, five and seven unit gang mowers, and of fine cut mowers for golf greens such as the Certes hand mower, and the Overgreen in 1939 which enabled one man to cut eighteen golf greens in one day.

The manufacturer of gang mowers continued throughout the Second World War to meet the demand for the cutting of airfields.

Post war, there was a rapid and dramatic quickening in the pace of change in society. The speed of technological

Ransomes Ajax production at Ipswich

Hydraulic 5/7 unit

Ransomes Matadors

innovation coupled with increased leisure time and a boom in sporting activities, drove Ransomes forward. New products for the home, for councils and local authorities, golf courses, sportsgrounds and open spaces were developed. Mowers such as the Ransomes Marquis and Matador were popular on large lawns and for those discerning customers who wanted a fine finish. High work-rate machines like the Hydraulic 5/7, the Motor 5/3 and the Motor Triple revolutionised high work-rate grass cutting.

DEFINING DECADES

The 1960's and 1970's were remarkable decades for Ransomes – and in particular for its Grass Machinery division.

Although Ransomes had a long tradition and a fine reputation for its farm machinery range of ploughs, combine harvesters, sprayers and drills, gradually sales of grass machinery began to dominate. By 1979, grass machinery accounted for half the company's sales, and by 1980 had passed the £20m mark.

In 1985, Ransomes bought Mountfield, the British manufacturer of rotary mowers to increase its foothold in the professional and domestic mower market. (the brand was later to be bought by an Italian company)

Then in 1987, a move that would been thought unthinkable to Ransomes' founders. The company sold off its farm machinery division to focus entirely on grass machinery. The same year, Ransomes Grass

Ransomes old and new

Ransomes Meteor

Ransomes mowers preparing a Swedish golf course

Machinery Division gained the Queens Award for Export Achievement. The transformation of the company was complete.

1998 saw Ransomes bought by the US industrial conglomerate, Textron Inc to complement their ownership of the Jacobsen range of grass machinery, and there were fears that production might cease at Ipswich after more than 200 years.

However, that has proved to be far from the case. The mower manufacturer plant at Ipswich is as busy, vibrant and innovative as ever, designing and manufacturing sophisticated mowing machines for use across the world.

As they have during the 19th, 20th and now 21st centuries, Ransomes continually innovate, seek solutions, problem solve and build machines for today and tomorrow. Edwin Budding would be absolutely delighted that the purchaser of his first licence are today still upholding the ideals and inspirations that spurred him on all those years ago.

Ransomes machine on company golf course at Ipswich HQ

Budding and **Ransomes**

Fast Mowers:
Man and machine

Any vehicle, be it car, motorcycle, quad-bike, truck – or lawnmower is capable of being taken to extreme performance levels.

Whereas the main purpose of a lawnmower is to sedately clip and roll the grass, there are those who see it as an opportunity to challenge man and machine. Lawnmower racing is an organised competitive sport. Engines are tuned, transmissions tweaked, seat and suspension eanhanced to see who can go fastest.

And then there is the quest to see how fast a mower can be propelled . . .

Pictured: Lawnmower racing in Sussex in 1995, mixing ride-on machines and those you have to push. Right in the middle of picture, Stirling Moss, in white helmet

Extreme Mowtoring:
The quest for speed

Lawn mower racing was started back in 1973 by an Irishman, Jim Gavin, who met with a bunch of friends one day at The Cricketers Arms in Wisborough Green, West Sussex. They were there for a few pints and to discuss their latest motorsport idea.

Jim was heavily involved in rallying at the time but saw the way that sponsorship was creeping in. He didn't really like this and wanted to create a form of motorsport that wouldn't involve lots of money and was readily accessible to everyone. As the beer flowed, they gazed across the village green to where the groundsman was mowing the cricket pitch. Which was when someone piped up "We've all got a lawnmower in our shed, lets race them!"

From those early days, the British Lawnmower Racing Association was formed.

The main objectives are no sponsorship, no commercialism, no cash prizes and no modifying of engines. The idea being, it would keep costs down and resulted in lawnmower racing being described by Motor Sport News as "the cheapest form of motorsport in the U.K."

The BLMRA still sticks to its origins as a non-profit making organization, any profits are given to charities or good causes.

Lawn Mower Racing takes place all over the country, normally from May to October. There are World Championships, a British Grand Prix, and the 12 Hour Endurance Race. Over the years lawn mower racing has

Don Wales in his record breaking run at Pendine Sands

attracted motor racing legends eager to try something different. Sir Stirling Moss won the BLMRA British Grand Prix and 12-Hour Race, as did Derek Bell, five times Le Mans winner.

DIFFERENT CLASSES
As with motor racing, there are different groups.

GROUP ONE
Group 1 is where lawn mower racing started. It is simple, easy, fun and exhausting! The group is based around the basic cylinder mower designed to cut grass for domestic purposes. It could be self propelled and roller driven. Only basic modifications are allowed to make these mowers go as fast as the operator can run, along with making them safe by removal or covering up of blades

GROUP TWO
Group 2 is for roller driven mowers of the cylinder type used with a trailed seat and often seen preparing cricket pitches, large lawns or sportsgrounds. In standard form it will be self propelled and roller driven but for racing it will have a towed seat. Competitors either use a tuned engine or un-tuned engine and maximum horsepower limits apply.

GROUP THREE
Group 3 is for four wheel garden ride-on mowers designed to mow domestic lawns, not sportsgrounds. These require a fair degree of preparation and potentially have top speeds in the order of 50 mph. They will have a chassis designed for an engine up to 18hp but with no obvious bonnet

GROUP FOUR
This group is for wheel driven lawn tractors. Similar mechanically to Group 3 with the obvious difference that they have a bonnet over a front mounted engine. They require a lot of preparation and also have a potential for 50 mph. Again the engine size will be up to 18hp and will have the engine situated in front of the operator with a rotary blade cutting deck suspended under the chassis

The 2014 12 Hour Endurance Race attracted 34 teams with the winning team covering 366 laps of the 1.37km course, over 312 miles, during the 12 hours most of which was in darkness. The race was officially started by Hollywood actress Julie Walters, and a course record was set by a team from Luxembourg who lapped in 1m 39 seconds at an average speed of 41.9mph.

The British Lawnmower Racing Association is believed to be the oldest such organisation in the world, but there is also competitive mower racing in the United States and in Australia.

Lawn Mower Racing

Media attention

LAWNMOWER SPEED RECORD
Extreme Mowtoring

On sunny weekend in 2010, one of those typically British challenges took place on Pendine Sands in Wales. It was the idea of Steve Vockins, from the National Motor Museum at Beaulieu whilst he was recovering from heart surgery.

"I wanted to do something mad, bad, and slightly dangerous," he said, "and have a tilt at the land speed record for a lawnmower of 80.69 mph set by American Bobby Campbell on a lawn tractor on Bonneville Salt Flats in 2006"

So Project Running Blade was born. He approached British garden tractor manufacturer Countax for their support to build a suitable machine, and driver Don Wales, a photographer by day but with speed in his blood. His grandfather Sir Malcolm Campbell, father of Donald Campbell, had broken the land speed record on Pendine Sands back in 1924.

But first, to be considered by the Guinness Book of Records, the Countax lawn tractor had to fulfill it's principal purpose and cut grass, so before the records attempt Don Wales mowed the lawn above the beach. Pic 006

A straight-line course covering almost the whole 4-mile stretch of Pendine Sands, provided plenty of opportunity for the specially prepared Countax lawntractor to get up to speed before passing through the one-mile timing section.

On the Saturday, a first run was completed with a roll-cage fitted, but even with the extra drag, Don Wales managed to reach 74 mph. After a couple of more runs, the roll-cage was removed and the lawn tractor made two runs at just over 84mph and 88mph - which claimed the record with an average of 86.09mph.

On Sunday, the team returned to Pendine, in front of a large crowd, with coverage on Sky News, eventually got in a flying mile just after 7.00pm which lifted the record once again to 87.33 mph. The pre-publicity had suggested

Final preparations

Record breaking team

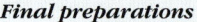

a target of 100mph but that was always more paper-talk than reality.

Even so, seeing and hearing the low-slung tractor streaking across the sand in the high-80s was a highly impressive sight and reward enough for the team that had made it possible.

The record had been regained from the Americans. However, just a few

Olivier Panis and Jarno Trulli pose with a pair of specially liveried Honda 2216 ride-on lawnmowers

months later, Bobby Campbell returned to Bonneville Salt Flats and regained the record with an official speed of 96.529, but then along came Honda . .

Mowing Mean Machine

Honda has a long history in virtually every branch of motorsport and powerboating. Formula One, Touring Cars, Motorcycles, Rallying, performance boats are all central to building the awareness of the Honda brand.

The company also has a wide range of mowers and garden equipment, so what more natural than they turn their attention to building a fast lawnmower? They had previously linked mowers with Formula One when a lawnmower race was staged at Silverstone inn 2004 with two Honda lawn tractors done up in the livery of the BAR-Honda team.

However it all got serious, when the Honda-prepared Mean Mower, a high-performance garden tractor set a new world record for fastest lawnmower in 2014 of 116mph (187kph).

Driven by Top Gear writer Piers Ward for the attempt, the 1000cc 109HP mower's average speed broke the previous record by almost 30mph.

The successful attempt took place at the IDIADA Proving Ground, in Tarragona, Spain'

As well as being required to cut grass and look like a lawnmower in order to fully satisfy and meet Guinness World Records rules, the mower had to record the same run, in both directions, within an hour – with the average speed taken of both runs.

The Mean Mower was designed and built in the UK by Honda (UK)'s British Touring Car Championship (BTCC) partner,

Team Dynamics. The team re-engineered a Honda HF2620 Lawn Tractor from the ground-up, adding an all-new fabricated chassis to provide a strong, safe, light platform. A 1000cc engine from a Honda VTR Firestorm motorcycle was used, along with bespoke suspension and wheels from a Honda All-Terrain Vehicle (ATV).

The cutter deck was custom-made in fibre-glass, to reduce weight, whilst the grass collector provided a place

116 MPH Lawnmower

for the fuel tank, oil cooler and a secondary water cooling radiator.

The mower can cut grass at around 15mph, thanks to two electric motors on the cutter deck, spinning at 4000rpm - more than double the flat-out speed of the original HF2620.

Helping with the design were two drivers from Honda's British Touring Car Championship, Matt Neal and Gordon Shedden. The mower has a six-speed gear system, a custom-made Cobra sports seat, special exhaust system - and a steering rack taken from a Morris Minor.

The result of this is a lawn mower set-up and geared to achieve a top speed in excess of 130mph, weighing just 140kgm - and an estimated acceleration of 0-60 of just four seconds!

Now that would have set Edwin Buddings juices flowing, that's for sure!

Bruno Senna aboard the Honda fast lawnmower

Budding's Legacy Series

Iconic lawnmowers that have shaped the industry

NUMBER 9: DENNIS MOWERS

Dennis started life at the end of the 19th Century when brothers Raymond & John Dennis set up in business together manufacturing motorised tricycles and cars in Guildford. In 1901 the two brothers set up Dennis Brothers Limited producing lorries, vans, buses and fire engines which were all in production by World War 1.

In 1922 the Dennis Motor Lawn Mower was announced. The company was already selling to local authorities so it was a logical step to make machines for public parks. By 1925 Windsor Castle was a Dennis Mower user as were many of the fine houses and estates around Great Britain. Mowers were exported around the world to every corner of the empire and beyond.

During World War II Dennis produced thousands of lorries, fire engines and a wide range of military equipment.

In 1945 the war was over and production of buses, lorries, fire engines and mowers picked up again.

But by the late 1950's the traditional Dennis Mower was becoming outdated relying on 1920's technology. New mowers were developed such as the Premier and Paragon as well as gang mowers. However, turbulent times during the 1960s resulted in Dennis deciding to focus solely on municipal vehicles and fire engines.

In 1976 the motor mower division was sold to one of its sub-contractors, whilst the gang mower division was sold to engineering company Howardson, who later bought the whole of the grass machinery division moving all the stock and production to Derby. New products were developed, and Howardson added Marathon Mowers and later the famed JP Mower business.

Today, the Dennis mower business is an important and growing division of Howardson who have considerably increased manufacturing capacity and strengthened its commitment to British manufacturing. Dennis mowers are used at leading sporting events around the world including venues for the FIFA World Cup.

"You have a problem in business or personal life. Take out the scythe and chances are, the answer will come to you"
Lord Deedes
writing in the Daily Telegraph

Quotes
... on lawns, lawn mowing and the meaning of life

Quotes

I spend hours mowing the lawn in absolute straight lines on my tractor. If it's not right, I do it again
Britt Ekland

... mow the lawn perfectly, but neglect to make the bed? It's pure, unadulterated logic. Everyone can see the yard - nobody can see the bed. The lawn is the canvas upon which guys judge each other. It's the great redeemer. If we aren't great lawn men, we're nothing.
Kevin Kerwin,
47 Husband Mysteries Solved.

There's one good thing about snow, it makes your lawn look as nice as your neighbour's
Clyde Moore

Mowing the grass has mind-body health benefits. There's something meditative about pushing a mower back and forth across that patch of green. Plus, it's a practical way to work in a workout while burning some serious calories.
Linda Wasmer Andrews,
Psychology Today

Grass is the cheapest plant to install and the most expensive to maintain.
Pat Howell

"The lawnmower is a symbol of potency because of all its "throbbing and thrusting in front of the male at approximately groin level"
Professor Halla Beloff

Quotes . . . on lawns, lawn mowing and the meaning of life

Until man duplicates a blade of grass, nature can laugh at his so called scientific knowledge
Thomas Edison

I wanted the influence. In the end I wasn't very good at being a president. I looked out of the window and thought that the man cutting the lawn actually seemed to have more control over what he was doing.
Warren Bennis
US Professor in Leadership Studies

I believe a leaf of grass is no less than the journey-work of the stars.
Walt Whitman

"Mowing the lawn, I felt like I was battling the earth rather than working it; each week it sent forth a green army and each week I beat it back with my infernal machine. Unlike every other plant in my garden, the grasses were anonymous, massified, deprived of any change or development whatsoever, not to mention any semblance of self-determination. I ruled a totalitarian landscape. . . . Another day it occurred to me that time as we know it doesn't exist in the lawn, since grass never dies or is allowed to flower and set seed. Lawns are nature purged of sex or death. No wonder Americans like them so much."
Michael Pollan

Hut doors open — check. Petrol levels topped — check. Oil gauge scrutinised, throttle to choke — check. You make sure your rotors are raised, your right foot is down on the clutch pedal. You turn the ignition and there comes that satisfying, chugging cough before the engine barks into furious action. It is at this moment that, sitting on my ride-on mower, I start humming the theme tune to Thunderbirds and reverse my riding mower out of her lair. Gently does it over that ramp. Then, after a final A-ok with my imaginary ground-staff and a word with International Rescue control tower, full revs! Or as the great Buzz Lightyear in Toy Story says: 'To infinity . . . and beyond!' You can tell a lot about a fellow's character from the state of his lawn. Time for dandelions and daisies to go to sleep with the fishes.
Time to mow.
Quentin Letts, Daily Mail 2014

Quotes . . . on lawns, lawn mowing and the meaning of life

Budding's Legacy Series

Iconic lawnmowers that have shaped the industry

NUMBER 10: LLOYDS MOWERS

Lloyd mowers started out as Lloyd, Lawrence & Company, founded by John Post Lawrence in 1878 as an agency for the import and sale of American "Pennsylvania" mowing machines in the City of London.

In 1913 John Lawrence decided that Letchworth would be an ideal new location for the company and so began the company's long and deep association with the First Garden City.

Production of the first Letchworth-made "Pennsylvania" professional mowers started in early 1934 and this was followed by the development and manufacture of a range of other compatible equipment.

The company is probably best known for its Lloyds Paladin Mower which has been in production for over 50 years. Introduced in 1961 to supersede the Lloyds Super Pegasus Mower which only had powered drive to the cutting cylinder. It was designed as a machine that would provide maximum cutting performance while making life more comfortable for the operator. Lloyds launched the Paladin at the National Association of Groundsmen Exhibition in 1961 and have exhibited a Paladin mower at every show since.

As a special landmark in 1977, Lloyds produced a totally silver Paladin in celebration of the Queens Silver Jubilee year. Manufactured from high grade aluminum, the components were

highly polished and all other steel parts were chromium plated. This unique machine was presented to Her Majesty and was used at Balmoral Castle.

During its 133 year history Lloyds and Co Letchworth remains a privately owned company with many of its employees having a vested interest in the company. It's mowers are used by many of the top sporting venues around the worlds, including many of the Test Match grounds.

PROFILE: BRITISH MOWER MAKERS

ALLETT: THE PROFESSIONAL'S CHOICE
The complete range for sportsground or fine turf

For 50 years, Allett mowers have been part of the UK's proud lawnmower heritage. A wholly British-owned company, which for 50 years, has specialised in the design and manufacture of precision-cut cylinder mowers, Allett has helped produce better, more consistent sports turf surfaces and finer ornamental lawns through ongoing technological advances

The first Allett prototype was a 36" wide machine designed, built and tested in 1965 by horticultural engineer, Reg Allett. A year later he had manufactured and sold his

Allett mowers at Anfield

first production mower.

Within two years of its launch, the Allett 36" was the professional groundsman's mower of choice and, by the late 1960s, these precision machines were cutting the outfields of every English Test Match venue and many county cricket grounds.

They were also trusted to prepare the pitches of leading football and rugby clubs and were specified for use at other sports venues, country estates and public parks throughout the UK, Ireland and continental Europe.

Throughout the 1970s, 80s and 90s, Allett continued to develop professional mowers with the introduction of the 20", 24", 30", 34" and 42" cut machines and by the early years of the 2000s, its professional cylinder mower range comprised specialist mowers for golf and bowling greens, sports stadiums, cricket wickets and outfields as well as public and private parks and gardens.

Allett was honoured when the Commonwealth War Graves Commission chose Allett mowers almost exclusively to maintain the grass within its immaculate cemeteries in Britain and all over the world.

NEW ERA

In August 2007, the company was acquired by the privately-owned Turfmech Group and Allett mower production was moved to Turfmech's state-of-the-art manufacturing centre in Hixon, Staffordshire who continued with Allett brand, so distinctive in the black, silver and gold livery, so recognisable throughout the world.

In 2011, a significant move saw Allett acquire the design and manufacturing rights to the former Atco and Suffolk Punch branded mowers from Bosch Lawn & Garden. These now form Allett's new "green and gold" Classic and Expert cylinder mower ranges.

The addition of the new Classic and Expert domestic and semi-professional cylinder mowers to its portfolio makes Turfmech the largest manufacturer of pedestrian petrol-engined cylinder mowers in Britain.

Today, the Allett brand of professional walk-behind cylinder mowers are leaders within their various market sectors, providing users with expertly-built, reliable, well-proven grass-cutting machines which produce a seemingly effortless first-class finish to every lawn on which they are used.

Mowing the pitch at Edgbaston

Profile: British Mower Makers

Lawnmowers in Advertising

Even from the early days, adverts for lawnmowers preferred featuring a woman behind the handles, presumably to demonstrate ease-of-use rather than any division of gender in mowing responsibilites

Lawnmowers in Advertising

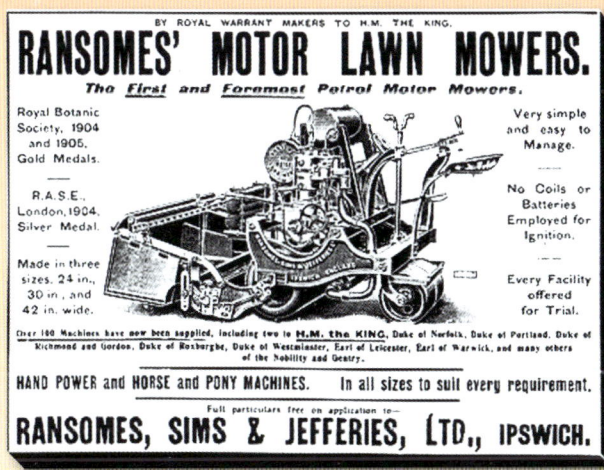

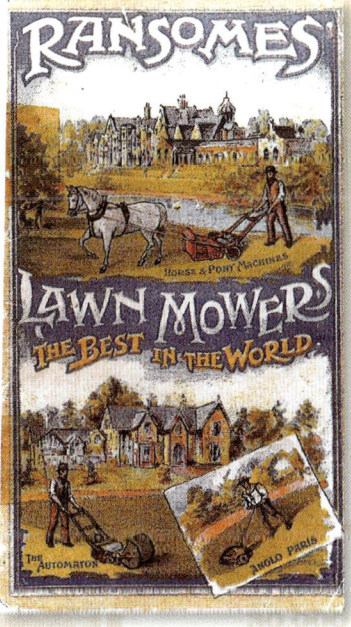

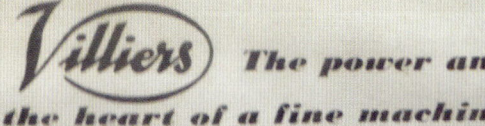

Lawnmowers in Advertising

The Great Lawnmower Advertising War

During the 1980s Flymo were all over the newspapers with adverts for their hover mowers demonstrated by girls in spangly jumpsuits, effortlessly trimming their lawn with sweeping strokes of floating Flymo.

Their strap line was simple **"It's a lot less bovver with a hover"**.

Their main rivals, Qualcast, manufacturer of the best selling Concorde called in Ron Collins, the adman behind the Cinzano ads, the "I'll bet he drinks Carling Black Label" campaign and BMW's Ultimate Driving Machine ad for BMW. Collins's devised a series of ads for Qualcast lawn mowers with his slogan **"It's a lot less bovver than a hover"**. A change of a single word.

The ad campaign was intensely fought out with TV ads and in the national press, and led to what the Sun newspaper dubbed "the Great Lawnmower War".

The peak came with a commercial depicting an actress pretending to make a standard Flymo ad, then getting the put-upon film crew to fix the damage the hover had wrought on her lawn by trundling the trusty Qualcast out of the shed and doing it properly, with nice regimental stripes and no clippings strewn everywhere!

All this made lawnmowing a strangely high advertising-spend sector back in the '80s, something that has not been repeated since.

Lawnmowers in Advertising

The American Dream

LEFT: Coca Cola advert featuring a Ransomes mower

RIGHT: Husqvarna advert for robot mower

Aspirational Advertising

These two adverts are the author's favourite advertisements from recent years and hint at exclusivity, aspirations and quality.

The Hayter advert, set in a picturesque garden with the strap-line **Country House by Sir Edward Lutyens. Lawnmower by Hayter** was a stunningly simple message, beautifully photographed. Another version was shot in the grounds of the terraced villas that surround Regents Park with the strap-line **Terrace by John Nash. Lawnmower by Hayter**.

Production costs for the campaign were high, as were the rates for placing the adverts in the quality newspapers. But it was time when Flymo and Qualcast were also spending a great deal of money on their 'Bovver' campaign, so other lawnmower manufacturers believed they could, or should, join in.

The **'Sir George' Dennis Mowers** advert played on issues of quality and heritage, perhaps harking back to the time when Dennis Mowers were used at Windsor Castle and at many stately homes around Britain. The advert from 1967 was designed at a time when Dennis, principally a manufacturer of lorries, buses and fire engines, was going through some turbulent times. The mower division was sold off and today production of Dennis Mowers continues at a factory near Derby.

Both adverts are now relics of their age, such aspirational advertising for lawnmowers is rarely seen today.

PROFILE:
BRITISH MOWER MAKERS

Best of British

Oxfordshire manufacturing base for leading garden tractor brands

The garden tractor has traditionally been the preserve of the huge United States market with its wide-open spaces and large lawns. Here in the UK however, we have a long and proud tradition of manufacturing ride-on mowers and lawn tractors ideally suited to conditions in this country.

Two names stand out, Westwood and Countax, as the only wholly British-made lawn and garden tractors. Today both brands are designed and manufactured in a modern factory in the heart of the Oxfordshire countryside.

agreed a deal with Oxfordshire neighbour, Williams Formula One to launch a Williams F1 garden tractor by Countax.

Westwood Tractors have been around for over 40 years having built models like the Lawn Bug and Gazelle which were some earliest British made ride-on mowers. Originally manufactured by Westwood Engineering based in Plymouth, the company became part of the Mountfield-Westwood group owned by Ransomes in 1990.

Countax Tractors was started in 1988 by an engineering entrepreneur, Harry Handkammer, whose company previously made various attachments for Westwood tractors. In the early 1990's, Handkammer lost the manufacturing contract so decided to build his own tractor, a decision that was see him awarded the title of Business Survivor of the Year in 1991 by the BBC's In Business programme.

The company designed and built the new Countax tractor from scratch, and by 1992 had claimed market leadership over its UK manufacturing rival, Westwood.

In 2000, Countax bought the Westwood business from Ransomes, so bringing together the manufacturing and marketing of the UK's only British-built garden tractors under one roof at the ever expanding factory at Great Haseley in Oxfordshire.

Always keen to be seen as innovators, Countax launched a special JCB-branded garden tractor in the famous yellow livery of the British manufacturer in 2003, and in 2008

NEW ERA

In 2010, Countax was acquired by the family owned US lawn and garden manufacturer Ariens Company. Based in Wisconsin, Ariens was founded in 1933 by Henry Ariens and his three sons, Steve, Leon and Francis, who developed the first American-made rotary tiller at a time when other manufacturers were experimenting with imported tillers.

The company grew over the years. Today it is regarded as one of the leading US manufacturers and is still in family ownership. The current chief executive is Dan Ariens, the great grand-son of Henry Ariens, and the fourth generation from the Ariens family to oversee future development. As wel as his many business connections, Dan is on the Executive Board of the Green Bay Packers NFL team.

The Countax Great Haseley factory is an example of modern manufacturing techniques and practices combining to build state-of-the-art products for todays consumers.

Dan Ariens

Profile: British Mower Makers

Earn Your Stripes!
Fields of dreams

Mowing is often an art-form. The striped effect of a lawn, golf course, football stadium or cricket ground is seen as enhancing the aesthetic and visual appeal. After all, Wimbledon wouldn't be Wimbledon without the stripes

The 'stripes' that you see are caused by light reflecting off the blades of grass. It has not been cut at a different height nor is it a different breed of grass. It is simply that the 'stripes' are made by the roller on the mower bending the grass in a different direction

When the blades of grass are bent away from you, the grass appears lighter in colour because the light is reflecting off of the wide, lengthy part of the blade. When the blades of grass are bent towards you, the grass appears darker as you are looking more at the tips of the blades (a smaller reflective surface) and the shadows under the grass.

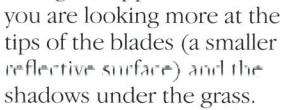

Striping a lawn can create a dramatic effect and elevate the lawn to a new level. When people refer to wanting their grass to look like a golf course, they usually mean the look of the striping rather than the health of the turf. Alternating mowing patterns by 90° or 45° adds to the aesthetic look - and is good for the grass.

Budding and Beer

By coincidence, the very year (1830) that Edwin Budding invented his lawnmower, the Government passed the Beerhouse Act, which abolished the beer tax, extended the opening hours of licensed public houses, taverns and ale houses to 18 hours a day.

The Government were keen to promote beer drinking instead of spirits, especially gin. Widespread drunkenness through gin consumption was believed to be detrimental to the working class and this had led to the rise of the Temperance Society which campaigned for closure of the 'gin shops'. The former drink of the working man: beer, was taxed which meant the cost of beer could be prohibitive to the working classes despite that fact that beer was safer to drink than water.

Within a few months over 24,000 beerhouse excise licenses were granted. The beerhouses provided not only beer, but food, games and some even lodging. In villages and towns many shopkeepers opened their own beerhouse and sold beer alongside their shop wares. Beer would be brewed on the premises or purchased from brewers.

The Wine and Beer House Act of 1869 changed the law brought licensing of the beerhouses back under the control of the local justices. Many then closed, or were purchased by breweries and changed to fully licensed public houses.

Whether Budding and his colleagues at Phoenix Iron Works were beer drinkers it is not known, but it is entirely apt that the site on which Budding came up with the idea for the lawnmower is now occupied by Stroud Brewery, whose very first beer was Budding Ale in 2006. The Budding Pale Ale, 4.5% ABV was the Champion Beer of Gloucestershire in 2006 and 2008.

It is described as "A popular pale ale with a grassy bitterness, sweet malt and luscious floral aroma, with Fuggles used as the main bittering hop – then late hopped for a luscious floral aroma. Our biggest selling beer!"

The founder of Stroud Brewery,

Greg Pilley, says "We are committed to using Cotswold grown and organic malting barley. We also strive for strong community bonds through projects such as Your Pint, Your Place, which aims to develop the relationship between the Brewery, its local community and the Cotswold farms that grow our malting barley"

BUDDING PLAQUE

The Stroud Brewery on the site of the Phoenix Iron Works is also the site of a Blue Plaque specially commissioned to commemorate Budding's achievement. The plaque was formally unveiled on 22 April 2015 by David Withers, President of Ransomes Jacobsen and David Hagg, Chief Executive of Stroud District Council

LAWNMOWER THEMED BEERS

A number of brewers have also brewed lawnmower themed beers in recent years. Presumably to try and replicate the evocative smell of newly cut grass –in a bottle. The **Lawnmower Amber Lager** is made by Falkenberg, a Carlsberg company

The George Wright Brewing Company on Merseyside brewed a special **Half-Cut Bitter** specially for the British Lawnmower Museum on 2011.

Look No Hands:

Robot mowers cutting away at the traditional lawnmower market.

It would surely have been an appealing challenge for Edwin Budding. His inventive mind would have loved to have used today's technology to design a machine to cut the grass with zero-effort.

After all, his original machine was heavy, cumbersome, difficult to move and need a man to push and man to pull.

The original design was soon improved upon to make operation much simpler with power added to propel the mower – and that progression has continued over the years.

However, in the post-war years, designers and developers started to think about the future. The Festival of Britain in 1951 started to peer into the future, the Festival's Dome of Discovery on London's South Bank highlighted areas of future science and technology.

In 1959, Birmingham-based Webb Mowers were invited to present their vision of the future at the Chelsea Flower Show as part of a wider presentation on the use of new technology in the garden.

Webb designed a prototype radio-controlled mower, which had a top speed of 2mph and was said to have a range of one mile.

The concept amused, but got no further. It also lacked much in the way of safety technology and it was quite possible for the operator to lose control and watch the machine dive into the bushes.

Early developments

It was another 40 years before automatic mowing, cutting the grass without an operator, started to become a commercial reality.

A typical robot mower requires the user to set up a border wire around the lawn that defines the area to be mowed. The robot uses this wire to locate the boundary of the area to be trimmed and in some cases to locate a recharging docking station, looking not unlike a dog kennel.

The machines employ sensors to avoid obstacles such as trees and lawn furniture and can safely reverse direction were they to bump into an inquisitive pet.

Some robot mowers move in random patterns, others follow distinct lines. They are designed to cut frequently, often daily. Because of this, robotic mowers don't collect the cut grass, their clippings are so small they break down quickly and act as fertiliser.

In the beginning, two companies were in the forefront of the race to develop robotic mowers that could appeal to gardeners - albeit at a price.

Husqvarna, the Swedish based appliance and engineering company, had started developing an automatic mower in the late 1980's using solar power. By 1995, the machine was ready to be marketed. It had cost millions in research and development and early machines cost £2000 each.

Meanwhile, in Israel, a small team of engineers led by entrepeneurs Udi Peless and Shai Abramson were also working on the robotic mower concept. Story is that Udi Peless' wife asked him to cut the lawn one day, not a chore that he enjoyed, so he started to think about doing away with the operator.

The Robomow used advanced robotic technology,

Husqvarna solar mower

Prototype radio controlled Webb mower (1959)

Look No Hands

Robomow founders Udi Peless (right) and Shai Abramson (centre standing) at Tel Aviv factory

much of which had been developed by the aerospace industry for use by the Israeli military.

Their company, Friendly Machines (later to be called Friendly Robotics), came up with the Robomow which was ready for the UK market in 1997 – at a starting price of under £1000. Again the development and marketing costs were enormous, but it is reckoned that the company sold around 4000 machines in the first five years. The company initially targeted the UK and employed a number of quirky methods to get the brand known, including a Robomow car which toured the country drumming up interest.

However, the set up and marketing costs were a considerable drain on the resources of the small Israeli company which subsequently had to be bailed out by Hoover for $2million. The interest from the giant home appliance company was driven by the prospect of developing robotic vacuum cleaners. Together, they used the Israeli mower technology to jointly produce one of the

Robomow promotional car

Honda Asimo robot with mower

Husqvarna Automower

first commercially viable robotic vacuum cleaners in 2003. Today, Robomow is again an independent company and competing in a crowded market.

Built in the UK

Between them Husqvarna and Robomow had done much of the hard work, but it took a further 20 years for other manufacturers to join in.

2013 saw a huge growth in the robotic mower market as well-known companies such as AL-KO, Bosch, Honda, John Deere, Stihl and Flymo (a sister company of Husqvarna) all introduced models. Honda had already started developing robotic applications including the humanoid robot, Asimo.

Sales took off in many European markets notably Sweden, Switzerland, France and Germany, but not necessarily in

Bosch robot

John Deere robot mower

sales are growing. For those with large gardens, who need to outside help, a robot mower can often replace the cost of a gardener. Improvements being added constantly. Special apps for programming the machines and smart phone technology are being used to improve the ease of control of the machines and to set mowing times.

Serious mowing

the UK, nor in the US where Husqvarna launched robot mowers in 2001 only to pull out a year later because of the over-abundance of inexpensive landscaping services meant Americans were just not interested in pricey machines.

Despite the reluctance of the UK to fully adopt robotic mowers, the largest manufacturing plant is here in the North East of England. Husqvarna, who are reckoned to be the market leader, manufacturer all their robotic mowers in the UK and its factory at Newton Aycliffe has recently produced its 500,000th robotic mower.

But the march of the robots is well and truly underway, with one market report saying that sales had risen 30 per cent in the past few years, but it still only represents just over 5% of the total lawnmower market.

With machines costing between £1500 and £2500, plus the cost of installing perimeter wires, buying a robotic mower is still a major purchase, but as each year passes

There are some areas of grass that require cutting, but that are often too steep for someone to use a mower safely. Motorway verges, ditches, inaccessible scrubland could well put an operator in danger.

So manufacturers have turned the clock back to the 1950's and that radio-controlled concept mower shown by Webb at the 1959 Chelsea Flower show.

For steep gradients, Ransomes market the Spider, a radio controlled four-wheel drive mower powered by a petrol engine. Used mainly by grasscutting contractors on motorway or roadside embankments or the sides of water reservoirs, the machine is controlled via a radio control box, will cut slopes up to 55 degrees and can swivel 360 degrees whilst cutting.

They are not cheap machines, the top of the range Spider costs over £33,000, with other smaller models still costing almost £10,000.

Walk or sit?

So if you don't fancy the exercise. If you regard mowing as a chore. You want to score a few points over your neighbour, then a robotic mower could be for you.

Relax in a garden chair, radio by your side, drink in hand – lift your feet as your mower glides by. Or watch from the window as your mower exits its 'kennel', the docking station, having taken on a new charge and wander around the garden for hours on end, cutting here, cutting there. Started to rain? Never mind, your mower will return to the docking station, take on a fresh charge and emerge when the rain stops.

Not sure that is exactly what Edwin Budding had in mind back in 1830 . . but as they say, that's progress. He would surely have been just as excited today as he was in 1830.

Ransomes Spider

ACKNOWLEDGEMENTS

Authors Note:
Much of the content in **The Budding Legacy** has been included in articles and photo features in my two magazines, **Service Dealer** and **Turf Pro** over the past 28 years. However, I am very grateful for the help, information, advice and support provided by so many people in the compilation of this book. They include:

Allett Mowers
Briggs & Stratton Corporation
Countax Ltd
Ransomes Jacobsen

David Withers, President of **Ransomes Jacobsen**

Stroud District Council
Museum in the Park, Stroud
Thrupp and Brimscombe Parish Council
Greg Pilley and all at **Stroud Brewery**

Brian Radam, **British Lawnmower Museum**
Andrew Hall, **Hall & Duck Trust**
Rochfords Garden Machinery
Paskett PR

All England Lawn Tennis Club, Wimbledon
Neil Stubley
Photo credits for pages 58-61
Matthias Hangst
Thomas Lovelock

Marylebone Cricket Club (MCC)
Mick Hunt
Clare Skinner
Sarah Williams and James Finlayfor Lords photos on page 67.

Gleneagles Hotel and Golf
Scott Fenwick

Real Madrid C.F.
Paul Burgess

The Groundsman magazine
Colin Hoskins for photos of Paul Burgess

Finally to . . .
Martin Hebditch for his design and artwork skills which beautifully compliment the content
and
My wife, **Trish Biddle**. Not only for her patience whilst I battled a tight publishing schedule, but for contributing the watercolour on page 92, based on early mower adverts

Who said lawnmowers were boring...!